The
STREET ROD

Tom Benford

MBI

This edition first published in 2004 by MBI, an imprint of MBI Publishing Company, Galtier Plaza, Suite 200, 380 Jackson Street, St. Paul, MN 55101-3885 USA

MBI titles are also available at discounts in bulk quantity for industrial or sales-promotional use. For details write to Special Sales Manager at Motorbooks International Wholesalers & Distributors, Galtier Plaza, Suite 200, 380 Jackson Street, St. Paul, MN 55101-3885 USA.

On the front cover: Although this '33 Plymouth Coupe—dubbed *Nasty* by owners Jim and Lucy McClusky—was neither chopped nor channeled, it has a low, clean look about it. It's a good idea to don sunglasses before taking a close look at the engine compartment—there's such a bevy of bright work there that it's almost blinding.

On the frontis: The dash of Ken Fenical's '32 Ford Deuce roadster is clean and uncluttered, almost to the point of being Spartan. Note the hand brake mounted on the floor at the right side of the transmission tunnel.

On the title page: Ray Slocum's chopped and channeled '35 Chevy two-door sedan looks like it's ready for action even when it's standing still. Ray's owned the car for over 17 years, and he has no plans of selling it.

On the back cover: Denny Buckley's '32 Ford highboy roadster is done right. Everything about the car—the engine, body, paint, and interior—works together well. All the "traditional values" of the early street rods, such as the dropped I-beam front axle, are present and accounted for here.

About the Author: A freelance writer and editor for more than 30 years, Tom Benford is a frequent contributor to *Vette, Corvette Fever, CorvetteMagazine.com, Corvette Enthusiast, Cars & Parts Corvette,* and *Cars & Parts Magazine.* Tom is the author of *Corvette Performance Projects (1968–1982)* (MBI), *The Corvette Encyclopedia* (Bentley Publishers), and *The Complete Idiot's Guide to Restoring Collector Cars* (Alpha/Penguin Books). He also shares author credit with Randy Leffingwell on *Corvette: Five Decades of Sports Car Speed* (MBI/Crestline Books). The Benford stable of old cars includes a '33 Dodge five-window coupe street rod and six Corvettes from the 1963 through 1981 years. Tom is a founding member of the *No Dice Cruisers,* a New Jersey-based car club that hosts its own annual charity benefit car show that attracts over 150 vintage, classic, street rod, and custom entries each year. Tom lives in New Jersey with Liz, his wife of 25 years, and their German Shepherd, Wolf.

Library of Congress Cataloging-in-Publication Data

Benford, Tom.
    The street rod / by Tom Benford
        p. cm.
    ISBN 0-7603-1793-3 (pbk.)
    1. Hot rods--United States. I. Title.

TL236.3B44 2004
629.228'6--dc22

Edited by Lindsay Hitch
Designed by Brenda Canales

Printed in China

Contents

Dedication

This book is dedicated to the memory of my close friend, fellow street rodder and true car nut, Roy Merkel (1952–2003). He lived the golden rule and enriched the lives of everyone who had the good fortune to know him. He passed away unexpectedly as this book was being prepared for printing.

Roy Merkel with daughter Elizabeth, Father's Day 2003.

Acknowledgments

As with any book of this nature, it could never have been produced without the time, effort, and cooperation of many good folks who generously made their American Street Rods available for me to photograph and provided me with specific information about their vehicles. I wish to extend a most sincere thank you to these good folks (alphabetically):

Liz Benford, Bricktown, NJ — '33 Dodge 5-Window Coupe
Denny Buckley, Marlboro, NJ — '32 Ford High Boy Roadster
Tony Castaldo, Neptune, NJ — '33 Plymouth 2-Door Sedan
Ken Fenical, Hummelstown, PA — '32 Ford Deuce Roadster/Posies Rods and Customs
Mike & Arlene Girard, Bensalem, PA — '37 Ford Coupe
Jim & Lucy McClusky, Edison, NJ — '33 Plymouth Coupe
Roy Merkel (posthumously), Manalapan, NJ — '36 International Truck
Ray Slocum, Wall, NJ — '35 Chevrolet 2-Door Sedan
Gary Van Wagner, Manchester, NJ — '37 Ford Cabriolet
Baron & Marion Yeager, Mercerville, NJ — '31 Chevrolet Coupe
Mike & Jackie Yencarelli, Neptune, NJ — '22 Ford T-Bucket

A very special thank you is in order for Dick Strom, who provided me with a wealth of information on hot rodding and the transition into street rodding. Muchas gracias, Dick.

I also want to thank Peter Bodensteiner, my acquisitions editor at Motorbooks International, for his faith in and support of this book.

And last, but certainly not least, I owe my heartfelt gratitude to my wife and best friend, Liz, for all her love, help, support, scheduling, proofing, encouragement, and photography assistance that made this book possible. I'm a lucky man, indeed, to have such a soul mate.

Introduction

I guess you could say I've been a car guy all my life. Even when I was a very young boy, I loved to build "soapbox" racers out of wooden boxes, some 2x4s, and the axles and wheels off an old carriage, using rope for steering gear. And, like the early hot rods that you'll read about shortly, very little thought was ever given to brakes for stopping these makeshift contraptions until after I kissed a tree or two when my downhill sprints came to an abrupt stop. But that was all part of the learning process.

Reflecting back, I also recall some of the stupid things I did in my teens, like removing the 4-speed trans from my Chevelle Super Sport so I could replace the clutch. I did the job right on the street in front of my house while the front of the car was supported only by a cinder block on one side and a bumper jack on the other.

Jack stands? We don't got no jack stands! We don't need no stinkin' jack stands!

My reasoning (in those days) was that with the money I saved on jack stands I could buy a couple of used tires at the junkyard. Hey, you gotta have your priorities in order, you know. Oh, the brash impertinence of youth.

I suspect a lot of my love of cars is hereditary. My dad raced stock cars until just before I was born, and he was a pretty good wrench, too, making money doing curbside repairs for folks as a sideline in addition to maintaining our own vehicles. He started collecting and restoring antique cars while I was still a young lad, and some of the best times I spent with my dad were the jaunts in his panel truck going to the boneyard in search of parts or tracking down a potential vehicle for restoration in some barn on the back roads of the East Coast. So it's pretty safe to say the apples didn't fall far from the tree. My brother, Tim, is also into old cars; he owns a 1956 Lincoln Mark II.

And while I was growing up the music of the Beach Boys, Jan and Dean, and numerous other recording artists certainly helped to reinforce the idea that cars in general were cool—and fast—flashy cars were even cooler. Songs like *Little Deuce Coupe* and movies like *American Graffiti* still evoke memories of those glory days of decades past.

But, thanks to street rods, those glory days live on. Every time I go for a cruise in our street rod, *Screaming Mimi*, the fire and excitement of driving something completely unique and cool is rekindled. The smiles on the faces of onlookers, the thumbs up and the OK signs they give me, and the admiring honks and headlight flashes from other motorists are always welcomed and appreciated. The acknowledgment that you're driving something very special is a rush you never tire of.

Street rodders are, in general, a congenial, gregarious, and fraternal bunch who willingly lend assistance, give advice, and share experiences with fellow rodders. I honestly believe there are no strangers in street rodding, just friends you haven't met yet. Liz and I have met folks who have become our closest and dearest friends over the years, and if it wasn't for street rodding, we never would have come into contact with these wonderful people.

Here in New Jersey, where I live, we're subject to seasonal changes and, more often than not, harsh winters. We only get about eight months of comfortable cruising weather each year and tend to cram as much fun time in as possible with our street rods.

You'll notice that several of the cars featured in this book have dual-purpose air conditioning and heater units installed. To a large extent, we East Coast street rodders are a hearty bunch and, as long as there isn't any snow or ice on the roads, we're game for cruising. To hell with the cold— let's go for a spin!

The important thing about all of the cars you'll be seeing and reading about here is that none of them are trailer queens. Each and every one of them is driven regularly and enjoyed by its owners, some of whom traveled quite a distance for my photo shoots. I enjoyed meeting these good folks, some for the first time, and I certainly hope you enjoy this book at least as much as I enjoyed writing it.

Street rodding has quite a colorful history, and it even has its own jargon. I've provided definitions within each chapter where applicable, and I've also included a glossary of 101 commonly used street rodding terms to help you understand what words such as "slammed," "shaved," "decked," and "channeled" mean when used to describe street rods.

Welcome to the wild and wonderful world of *The Street Rod*. Buckle up—you're in for quite a ride!

CHAPTER ONE

The Evolution of Street Rodding

Well, one thing's for sure: street rods owe their existence to the good old American hot rod. Sometimes the line between a hot rod and a street rod is blurred; other times it is crystal clear.

Hot rods were generally built for speed, which means their engines were souped up and things like fenders, engine hoods, running boards, and other nonessential items were taken off the cars in an effort to save weight and help increase their speed.

Webster's Dictionary defines the term "hot rod" as "an automobile rebuilt or modified for high speed and fast acceleration," noting that the term was already in general use by 1945.

Dick Strom, who's been a dyed-in-the-wool street rodder from way back when they were still called hot rods, pointed out to me that *Webster's* "hot rod" definition is sandwiched between "hot pursuit" ("... close

Except for the wild paint job, the Weld racing wheels, and the absence of front and rear bumpers, Baron and Marion Yeager's '31 Chevy Coupe looks pretty stock. Even the soft top has been retained to help keep the resto rod look.

continuous pursuit of a fleeing suspected lawbreaker") and "hots" ("... a strong sexual desire, as in he (or she) has 'the hots' for someone").

Conversely, a street rod is defined as a modernized vintage automobile. The car must have been manufactured in or before 1948. Street rods are usually decorated with colorful paint and have plush interiors. Many include modern features, such as four-wheel disc brakes, air conditioning, cruise control, tilt steering, and exotic stereo systems.

Hence, it would seem that while the hot rod was built solely for speed, the street rod is built for looks, comfort, and high performance.

Always Trying to Build a Better Mousetrap

The important thing to remember is that folks have been modifying their vehicles for increased performance or unique appearance virtually from the time the first internal combustion engine tenaciously fired and belched out exhaust gas. More frequently than you'd imagine, many of these improvements and modifications were the result of serendipity rather than engineering research and development.

The history of street rodding is a bit murky to say the least, unlike other areas of automotive history that have been very well documented by the major manufacturers, racing enthusiasts, and others who approached recording them in a scholarly fashion. But that's because those who were unknowingly creating street rod history were too busy building their unique vehicles to bother recording what they were doing for posterity. These guys were the purists—with a wrench in one hand and a torch in the other, their vision was clear and their desire was to create cars that suited their particular tastes and designs.

Today, thanks to numerous publications and national organizations like the National Street Road Association (NSRA), street rodding's ongoing history is now very well documented. But let's digress back into yesteryear to get a glimpse of what it was like back then, to give you a better idea of where it went and how street rodding got to where it is today.

A Sordid Past, Indeed

The hot rodding craze really started when Ford released its flathead V-8 engine in 1932. Right from the get-go, guys started tweaking this mill to coax more horsepower out of it for several reasons, not the least of which was for running illicit whisky and bathtub gin during Prohibition. Infamous personas such as Bonnie and Clyde and other ne'er-do-wells of the era plied their trade using Ford V-8-powered cars to make their getaways.

Early on, the term "hot rod" took on an unsavory connotation that evoked images of irresponsible young men racing around the streets in their loud, rude, and crude jalopies terrorizing the general populace with no regard for property, life, or limb. Intoxicated on speed, these hot rodders felt the streets were as good a place as any to race. Their vehicles were jerry-rigged to go fast and little thought was usually given to stopping them; structural integrity was scarcely given much, if any, consideration. Hot rodders were hell-raisers, pure and simple.

After Prohibition was repealed, but still prior to World War II, young men with a mechanical flair frequently engaged in street racing, usually at night, using the cloak of darkness to aid and abet their illegal activities. When the local constabulary did catch these hell-raisers in the act they would attempt pursuit of the lawbreakers. But their black-and-white police cruisers were hardly a match for the high-powered, stripped-down hot rods or the maniacal drivers who piloted them. This was an era of one-on-one pursuit—the good guys chasing the bad guys—and there was no modern radio communication that would have enabled interaction and coordination between police cars. Everything went through the radio dispatcher in those days, so giving chase was the only game in town for law enforcement.

The "Wrenches" Go to War

With the onset of World War II, many hot rodders were pressed into duty overseas working on the maintenance of military vehicles. This proved to be a great educational opportunity for them since they learned new speed tricks from one another and honed their skills at building and modifying engines.

After serving their hitches, they returned to civilian life and picked up right where they left off, but now they had the added assets of their muster-out pay to invest in making their rods even hotter and faster. And where better to test these hot new improvements than right back on the same streets they had already raced on?

From a full frontal view the resto-rod look is apparent. The gold-toned trim provides a nice touch against the chrome of the bumper and grill, and it's carried through on both of the side mirrors as well. Note the amber turn signals tucked below the fenders.

This resulted in hot rodders getting an even worse rap than they had before the war, and deservedly so. With gasoline running through their veins and horsepower on their brains, these crazies were a blemish on the face of their communities, a danger and a curse to law-abiding citizens, and the scourge of law enforcement. Songs like *Hot Rod Lincoln* and movies like *Hot Rods to Hell* and *Thunder Road* served to spread and reinforce the negative image of hot rodders as hell-raisers, malcontents, and irresponsible hoodlums.

A Menace to Society

Just the way the Hells Angels, the Pagans, and other "outlaw" motorcycle gangs gave Harleys and motorcycling in general a bad name and dark image in society a few decades ago before, hot rodders were generally regarded as social misfits, disdained by decent folk. There were undoubtedly those who built safe hot rods and drove them sensibly, but they too were cursed with the stigmata of the hell-raisers.

My mom used to have an expression, "Show me your friends and I'll tell you what you are," which had some merit and truth to it. With these early hot rodders, it was more a case of, "Show me what you drive and I'll tell you what you are." If you drove a hot rod, regardless of whether you were the good, the bad, or the ugly, you were a hell-raiser and shunned by society. That's just the way it was—at least at first.

The 4.5-inch top chop and 15-inch rear wheels contribute significantly to this car's rake. All you'd need to complete the "period" feel are a couple of round portholes in the rear quarter with Tommy-gun muzzles sticking out. What a rum-runner this rod would have made during the Prohibition period.

Testosterone on the Tarmac, Not the Streets

Before World War II began, those with the need for speed took to the Bonneville salt flats and several dry lake beds in California and neighboring states to get their go-fast jollies. The big attraction of these unpopulated vast expanses was plenty of space to open your engine up and lots of room to come to a stop after your run. Timed runs on measured-mile courses were recorded and eventually these turned into land speed record attempts, with records routinely set and broken by even faster vehicles on a regular basis.

Then, after World War II ended, the runways used to train B-17 and B-29 bomber pilots were abandoned, since they were no longer needed. No one seems to remember who it was exactly, but somebody came up with the bright idea of converting them into drag strips. These runways-come-drag strips were used as relatively safe straight-aways where these guys could vent their testosterone and stomp the pedal to the metal without putting innocent folks at risk. The idea caught on, slowly at first, and gradually gained momentum. While it didn't eliminate street racing totally, it did help to reduce it quite a bit.

But even so, both the bad rap and the bad rep of hot rodders remained, refusing to die despite the efforts of such well-established groups as the National Hot Rod Association (NHRA) to put a positive public relations spin on the hobby/sport. The bad image was all but impossible to ditch. Some new strategy and positive spin were needed badly.

The Cavalry Cometh: Enter the NSRA

The National Street Rod Association was formed in 1970 with the goal of burying the unsavory image and lurid past of hot rodding. The overall objective of the fledgling organization was to create a positive public attitude toward rodders by encouraging them to get their act together. Members of car clubs and "lone wolf" rodders alike were encouraged to show respect to law enforcement and to extend courtesy to fellow motorists.

NSRA members were also encouraged to assist stranded motorists and to get involved positively in their communities. Many local car clubs gave their members "courtesy cards" to identify themselves as members when they provided roadside help. And the newly coined term "street rod" also provided some additional distance and dissociation from the negative connotations that "hot rod" bore.

The NSRA was the organizing body that made the hobby/sport what it is today. Without a doubt, the NSRA is the reason the growth of street rodding has continued at a steady pace since its inception. The organization provides "leadership, guidance, and fun events for enthusiasts who favor driving their specialty cars wherever and whenever they want to."

Currently boasting more than 60,000 members from all over the United States, Canada, Australia, the United Kingdom, Germany, Mexico, and Sweden, the NSRA also elaborates on the definition of what a street rod is:

An automobile of 1948 or earlier manufacture which has undergone some type of modernization, to include any of the following: engine, transmission, interior refinements, and any other modifications the builder desires. A street rod is to be driven to events under its own power and is to be used as a safe, non-racing vehicle for total family enjoyment.

Additionally, according to the NSRA, a street rod is a means of self-expression for its creator. The builder of a street rod isn't confined to guidelines set down by someone else; he can be his own man and the street rod can be whatever he wants it to be, as long as the basic vehicle was manufactured prior to 1949. The street rod builder can add a late model engine and drive train from any make of car, modify the suspension to give better ride and handling characteristics, and incorporate whatever creature comforts he wants. Air conditioning, cruise control, AM/FM stereo radios and CD players, power steering, power brakes, power windows, and automatic transmissions are common. The end result is an automobile tailored to the owner's wants that still retains the looks and charm of a vehicle 50, 60, or even 70 years old.

A street rod builder can also use as mild or as wild a paint theme as he desires and can modify the lines of the body to suit his own tastes. The sky is the limit, and he can do whatever he wants without worrying about standards set down by someone else.

The Rush is in the Ride

There's no question that some folks enjoy building a street rod and, after it's finished, sell the vehicle so they can start another street rod building project. Not everyone can build a street rod, and it's folks like these who supply the street rods for those who can't.

I and many other street rod enthusiasts find that one of the best parts of owning a street rod is not in the creating of a unique vehicle, but rather in its enjoyment after it is completed. With the modernization comes the ability to enjoy the vehicle in ways other resurrected old cars can not be. The vehicle can be driven for long distances in comfort, with safety to the passengers and others on the highway. In addition to making the car more comfortable, improvements in steering, lighting, and brakes are nearly always included in the building of a street rod.

A street rod is a nostalgia trip and, while it retains most of the appeal of an old car, it is a venue for self-expression that allows the creator to incorporate his own ideas in paint, body work, and the mechanics that make it go. In this era of special interest automobiles, the street rod is one of the truest forms of personalized vehicles, and many street rods are forms of kinetic modern art.

Rolling Sculpture

Many street rods can rightly be called rolling sculpture. They are automotive art forms that showcase the talent, imagination, craftsmanship, and creativity of the owner and/or builder. The great thing about street rods, however, is that they can be driven and enjoyed, rather than just admired.

Street rodding is enjoying unprecedented growth, particularly among baby boomers. Now, with more disposable income and leisure time available than in years past, these folks can afford to build safer and better-looking street rods replete with just about every conceivable creature comfort. This has most certainly improved the visual image of the sport/hobby and made it more acceptable in the public eye.

Although many fine street rods have been built for far less, the average street rod costs somewhere in the $30,000-$50,000 range to build, and some professionally built rods are in the half-million-plus range.

It's really not a money thing, however. You can go out and buy a street rod, but that doesn't make you a street rodder. Street rodding is a state of mind—it's more of a Zen thing. A street rodder forms an intimate alliance with his vehicle—he and the rod become one enraptured entity. And that's what makes owning and driving a street rod so different from mundane, "normal" cars.

No Longer Crude and Rough

Today's street rods are a far cry from the early rods that tore up the streets and high school parking lots a few decades ago. Thanks to a bevy of specialty manufacturers, you can get the very best parts and components for increasing performance, handling, comfort, and safety in a street rod. Without a doubt, many street rods today are at least as good as many of the vehicles Detroit cranks out—some are even better, since they're assembled from the best of original equipment manufacturer (OEM) products and top-quality aftermarket items.

It's not uncommon to see street rods sporting Jaguar or Corvette independent rear suspensions, Camaro front sub frames, Mustang II independent front suspension, and dropped I-beam solid or tube front axles. Transmissions run the gamut from three-on-the-tree to four-on-the-floor or automatics, and some even have overdrive for highway cruising.

Others offer conventional steering with drum juice binders, power rack-and-pinion steering with four-wheel power discs, and anything from single carburetors to multiple carbs with blowers or fuel-injected engines. There is no limit on the amount of ingenuity and engineering you can put into a street rod—literally anything goes.

Cabin accoutrements such as power windows, air conditioning, multispeaker stereo systems with multidisc CD changers and graphic equalizers, tilt-telescopic steering wheels, rearview mirrors with electronic compass and outside temperature indicators built in, and more, are frequently found in today's street rods. Color-screen GPS units, DVD players, and even Nintendos are installed in street rods to keep the kids (or grandkids) happy when taking the family out for a cruise.

Seating can range from a molded fiberglass racing seat with a minimal amount of padding and a five-way harness all the way up to six-way adjustable power seats with lumbar supports upholstered in the finest leather. You'll see cloth and Naugahyde bench seats, contoured buckets, and other seating configurations as well. As with all aspects of street rodding, variety is the spice of life.

As far as exterior finishes go, you're liable to see everything from the retro hot rod look of gray primer to multistage pearl, metallic, and metal-flake paint jobs and iridescent finishes that change color as you change your viewing angle. You'll see scallops, flames, splash, shredding, and "ghost" effects like flames that only become visible at certain angles.

Ground effects are popular with street rodders, too. Neon license plate frames and neon tubes affixed to the undercarriage give street rods a nighttime glow all their own. LED license plate bolts and tire valve stem lights, fluorescent light rings that backlight the disc brakes, strobes, and other lighting effects are all used to make unique street rodding statements.

Talking the Talk

Street rodding has its own jargon, too. You'll hear terms used to describe changes rodders routinely make to set their cars apart from the mainstream. A few of the more common terms are:

Chopped—Lowering the roof of a hard-top car.

Cream-colored genuine leather buckets, door panels, and headliner give the car's interior a clean look. Flush, oval billet, inside door release handles help to keep the door panels uncluttered.

Channeled—Cutting the floor so the body rests around the frame rails rather than sitting on top of the frame to give an overall lowered appearance.

Sectioned—Removing a horizontal section of bodywork to lower the overall height of the body.

Raked—Lowering the front end of the car more than the back. This can also refer to a slanted windshield.

Nosed—Chrome details and trim removed from the hood and smoothed over.

Decked—Chrome details and trim removed from the trunk and smoothed over.

There are several genres of street rods, and there's something for just about any taste you could think of.

Here's a small sampling of the kinds of street rods you'll see at cruise nights and car shows:

Resto rods or **sleepers**—these rods look original on the outside but have all kinds of performance modifications under the hood and in the cabin.

Nostalgia rods—these have the retro look of the hot rods of the past. These are sometimes finished in gray primer or black sealer and may have wide whitewalls mounted on chrome or painted reversed steel wheels. They may have spun aluminum wheel discs, spinners, or flipper wheel covers, a pair of fuzzy dice hanging from the mirror, a Lady Luck shift knob, and a suicide knob on the steering wheel—the whole nine yards to invoke memories of Ricky Nelson's rod on the old *Ozzie & Harriet* TV show.

Techy turn-key rods—these are top-drawer, expensive vehicles built by professional rod builders. These rods usually have all of the best-available engineering components such as hydro-formed frame rails, Cadillac North Star power plants, On Star systems, and other state-of-the-art features. More often than not, these rods cost six figures.

Lead sleds—these are also nostalgia vehicles that have had their fender seams and other joints filled in (traditionally with lead solder, hence the name) to smooth them out. They're usually lowered and have frenched headlights and tunneled radio antennas.

Highboys—these are usually fenderless early Fords but they can be other makes as well. The name derives from the fact that they sit at the same height as the original stock vehicle.

Labor-of-love rods—you'll see lots of these since they're the pride and joy of the build-it-and-drive-it street rod set. More often than not they're "works in progress" as additional changes are continually made to improve the vehicle.

And that is both the essence and beauty of street rodding: the freedom to build and drive whatever it is that appeals to each rodder on his or her own personal level. And as long as you like what you've built and what you drive, it matters not what others may think. That's what street rodding is all about—gettin' in and gettin' it on.

This full side shot of the car shows its forward rake. The Chrysler torsion bar front suspension makes it easy to adjust the front ride height, so the rake can increase or decrease on a whim if the driver wishes to do so.

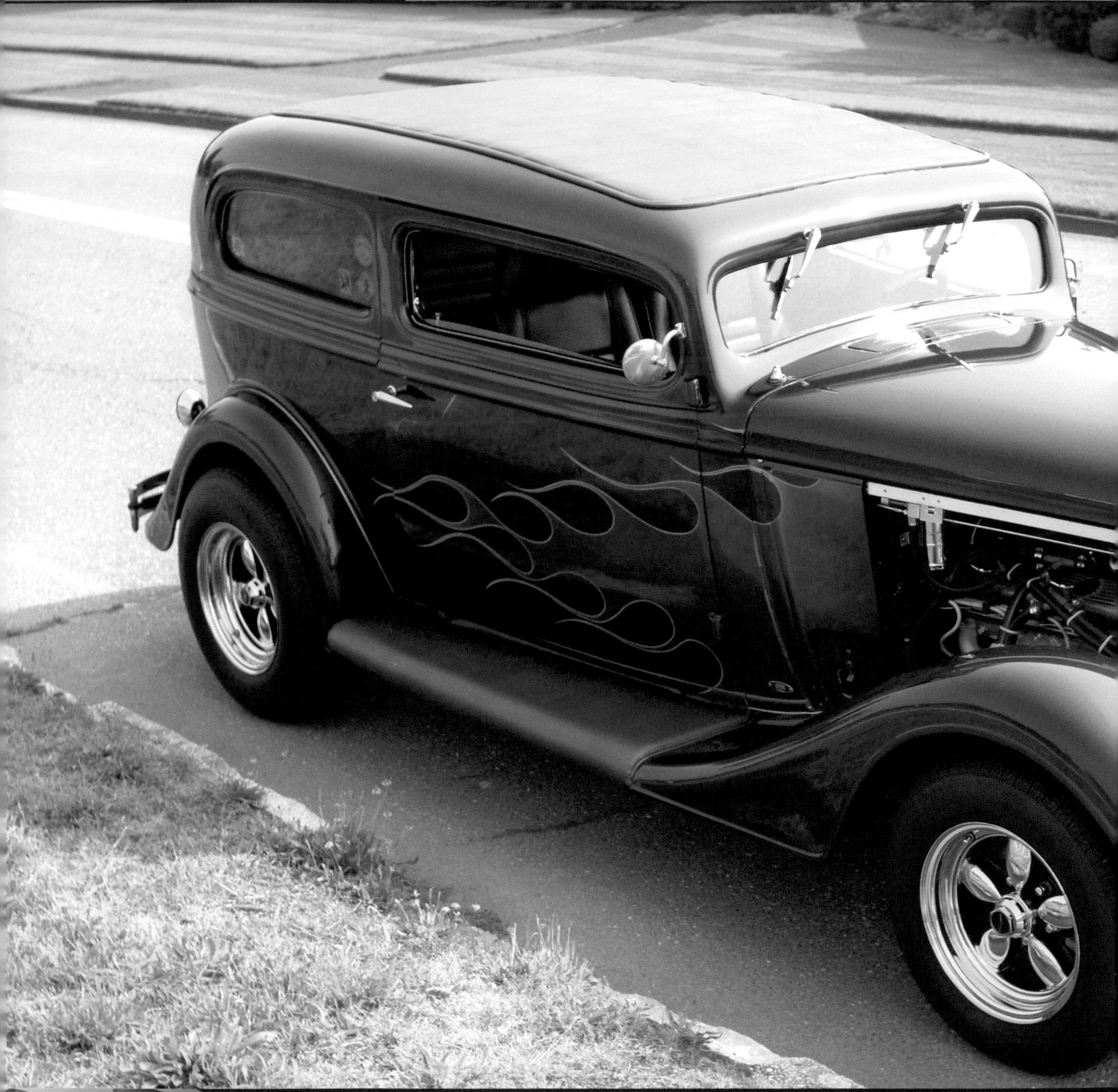

CHAPTER TWO

Low 35

1935 Chevrolet Two-Door Sedan

Ray Slocum describes his cool ride as "an older type of street rod," confiding that he's "from the old school, I guess you could say, and I'm very comfortable with the way the car is." He must be, owing to the fact that he's owned the car for over 17 years. Even though it was a street rod when he bought it, he's had it apart several times, making various changes or improvements along the way to make it suit his tastes. The body is all steel, although he installed fiberglass fenders on the rod about 10 years ago. The car originally came from Iowa, but it's been a resident of the Garden State for almost two decades now.

The green flames against the darker green body endow *Low 35* with a very distinctive look. Even though Ray says the rod is "old school," it works just fine, especially since the "retro look" is making a big comeback in street rodding.

The 350 Bowtie motor has a .030 overbore and a radical cam. A 600 cfm Holley feeds the beast, and Jet Hot block-hugger headers route the exhaust gases to the dual exhausts. Green anodized billet filler caps and green plug wires and wire looms keep the "green theme" going throughout the entire car.

The power is supplied by a small block Chevy mill bored .030 over, equipped with a fairly radical cam and fed by a 600 cfm Holley carburetor.

Cam—This refers to the camshaft, a shaft in the engine which is driven by gears, belts, or chains from the crankshaft. The camshaft has a series of cams, or lobes, that open and close intake and exhaust valves as it rotates.

CFM—This is an abbreviation for Cubic Feet per Minute, which is a measurement of the volume of air a carburetor can induct. The higher the CFM, the richer the air/fuel mixture, resulting in more horsepower.

The power train consists of a "worked" Turbo Hydramatic 350 trans with a shift kit installed that connects to an early '70s Corvette IRS rear end with 3.71:1 gearing.

IRS—This is an abbreviation for Independent Rear Suspension. IRS setups from Corvettes and Jaguars are sometimes used on street rods rather than "solid" rear axles.

When Ray decided to overhaul the engine about a decade ago, he made some other improvements including the installation of block-hugger headers with silver Jet Hot powder coating.

Even the fuel-filler neck has an upholstered bib to prevent any spills from hitting the pristine metallic green paint job. The gold-tone accent trim can be seen on the taillight.

Headers—Fine-tuned tubular steel exhaust manifolds that are more efficient than stock cast-iron manifolds. They are usually chromed or powder-coated.

A more recent modification was the installation of a three-piece Rootlieb engine hood with Dan Fink hardware holding it all together. Ray said that getting the hood, hinging, and supports to fit right was a real bear of a job; between mounting the hood, setting up the hardware, and painting the hood to match the rest of the car, he and his cohorts put over 100 hours into the project. The sides of the hood are removable for showing off the engine and for promoting better airflow in hot weather.

You don't usually think of upholstery on the outside of a car, but this one has plenty of it. In addition to the roof panel, the running boards sport upholstered pads, the fuel filler has an upholstered bib, and the spare-tire cover bears out some fine needle work as well. The same green theme used for the body is carried through on the upholstered components also.

Running Board—The metal strip running between the fenders and below the doors of early autos and trucks used as a step or to wipe one's feet before entering the vehicle.

Viewing the car full-on from the side lets you appreciate how much the top was chopped. Unlike many other cars of this era, this Bowtie has standard-opening doors rather than suicide doors. Ray has all of his NSRA membership stickers affixed to the window behind the driver's seat, which also has a rose etched into the glass.

To give the car the bad-ass stance and low look it has, the roof was chopped 4 inches and the body channeled 2 inches over the frame. Larger tires at the rear also contribute to the rake that gives this ride some attitude.

While Ray originally had true wire-spoke wheels on the car, he opted to change over to the original American Racing "Coke bottle" wheels the car now sports. He bought the used wheels several years ago from a friend who had used them on his 1934 Ford street rod. The price was right, so Ray snatched them up.

To keep the passenger compartment comfortable, air conditioning was a must. Ray had a Vintage Air system installed and it's proven to be a good investment for some of the 500-plus mile jaunts he has taken the car on. He describes the car as "very reliable and comfortable," although he admits that he doesn't get very good gas mileage, which he blames in large part on the radical cam he's running. That, coupled with the fact that the car has only a 12-gallon gas tank, makes refueling stops a frequent occurrence on any long road trip.

The gold-rimmed Stewart-Warner gauges give the dashboard a traditional look, and an AM/FM/cassette stereo system mounted there provides the cruising music. The comfortable bucket seats came from a Pontiac Fiero, salvaged from a boneyard.

Both the exterior and interior of the car sport gold-toned components, which gives a complementary contrast to the chrome trim items.

The gold-rimmed Stewart-Warner gauges keep Ray abreast of what's going on under the hood, while an AM/FM/cassette stereo provides the road music. Ray's a practical guy, so when it came time to do the interior, he had map pockets installed on the door panels, which he uses regularly. The two knitted sponge dice suspended from the rearview mirror have 3s on all the faces of one and 5s on the other.

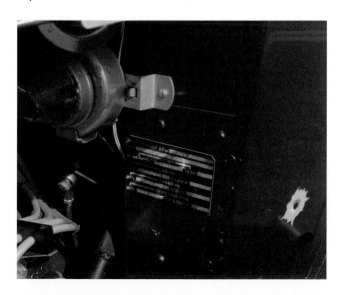

While Ray dubbed the car *Low 35*, it is certainly at the top of his favorite vehicle list.

Suicide Door—A door that hinges at the rear and opens from the front.

An engraved plaque mounted on the firewall provides all the vital statistics of the car. The bullet-hole decals are there "just for fun," Ray says.

CHAPTER THREE

The Wild One

1937 Ford Coupe

Mike Girard wanted a street rod with "attitude" and that's what he set out to build. He always thought the 1937 Ford Coupe had lots of attitude to begin with, so that was the basic platform he started with. He had some wild ideas of what he wanted the car to look like and, eventually, when it all came together, he dubbed the car *The Wild One*.

The all-fiberglass body came from Wild Rodz and it sits atop a Johnson's Rod Shop frame. The paint is a custom-mixed, two-tone bronze and copper from Sikkens, with custom graphics and a "leopard spot" motif in keeping with the "wild" theme. The metallic bronze and copper are separated by a thin beltline stripe that runs the full length of the car.

The car sits very low thanks to the Air Ride Technologies adjustable suspension at all four corners; the car can be dropped even lower than it was here and then raised to a more comfortable height for driving. American Racing Torq Thrust II wheels with Dunlop rubber all around contribute to the car's "attitude."

The "leopard spot" graphics and custom striping theme is consistent throughout the car, both inside and out. The beltline stripe serves to separate the metallic bronze from the metallic copper in the overall paint scheme.

Beltline—The line running around a car's body formed by the bottom edges of the side windows.

Mike wanted the rod to have plenty of get-up-and-go, so the engine choice was a Corvette LT-1 350-ci power plant outfitted with an LT-4 hot cam and roller rockers. For additional underhood eye candy, Street & Performance dress-up goodies were added.

CI—A measurement of the volume of an engine's cylinders in cubic inches that denotes the total volume of the engine's combustion chambers. Essentially, the larger the ci, the more horsepower the engine can produce.

A 4L60 automatic trans delivers the power to the rear wheels via a 10-bolt Chevy positraction rear end with 3:00 gears. Mike deliberately selected the

3:00 gearing so that he could cruise along without making the engine work hard. Apparently, he did it right, since the car boogies at 65 miles per hour while only winding 1,400 rpm. Mike also claims the car gets great gas mileage, another plus of the 3:00 rear-end ratio.

The suspension is from Air Ride Technologies at all four wheels and the car sits very low. Stopping power is provided by four-wheel discs with polished four-piston calipers by Wilwood Engineering. The rolling stock consists of the very popular American Racing Torq Thrust II wheels with 17x8s at the front and 20x10s at the rear, all wearing Dunlop SP 9000 tires.

Mike outfitted the rod's interior with cream-colored leather bucket seats, a custom console, and a headliner. He went with a Prowler-style dash using

A Corvette LT1 engine with an LT4 cam and other performance mods provides the go-power. The judicious use of chrome, polished stainless, and polished billet aluminum components, as well as braided stainless hoses, give the engine compartment just the right amount of eye candy without going overboard.

gold-trimmed Auto Meter analog gauges that give it a retro look. The "leopard spot" motif carries through on the upper door panels, and the leather theme continues into the trunk. Flush oval aluminum interior door release handles keep the door panels looking smooth and unobtrusive. Since the doors are solenoid-activated by remote control,

there are no exterior handles to detract from the car's smooth lines.

The car doesn't come up short on creature comforts, either. Air conditioning from Vintage Air keeps the cabin cool, while a polished Ididit tilt steering column and a Billet Specialties steering wheel make the piloting a breeze. There's a remotely

The Billet Specialties steering wheel and the Ididit tilt steering column with billet drop mount work well together. Mike chose the gold-trimmed Auto Meter gauges mounted on a Prowler-style dash to trick out the interior, combining current custom technology with a retro look. Billet gas and brake pedals complete the polished aluminum hardware. Note the striping at the top of the dash and on the console—first class all the way with this car.

operated Secret Audio stereo system with a six-CD changer in the trunk. Remote controls also open and close the trunk and windows.

An electrically operated hood provides access to the Corvette engine, and a stainless steel exhaust system evacuates the spent fuel gases. The rear license plate, suspended just in back of the rear end, is only visible if you view the car from a low level at the rear. Mike confides that the local constables often hassle him about it but, luckily, he hasn't been given any citations yet. When he explains that the plate would ruin the clean, uncluttered rear and he gives them the five-minute tour of the car's goodies, the police usually concur and get off his case.

Mike Girard wanted a car with "attitude," and *The Wild One* has it big-time. The absence of outside door handles or other obtrusions gives the car an extremely clean and smooth look. Remote-controlled solenoids are used to pop the doors open. This is one '37 Ford Coupe that's been done right, for sure.

The trunk is finished in cream-colored leather and the six-CD changer is nestled unobtrusively in there as well. Selecting tracks and changing discs is done with a remote control mounted in the console.

The absence of visible taillights and the "cyclops" brake light also contribute to the clean look of the car. The taillights and the brake light are actually concealed by a light coat of paint, but they are indeed visible when the light switch is in the "on" position or the brake pedal is applied.

Mike drives the car to shows, where it is a consistent trophy winner. He says it wouldn't be very wild if he trailered it, and who could argue with that?

The clean, uncluttered rear continues the smooth lines of the car around back. The license plate is only visible if you kneel and look under the car, which occasionally provokes hassling by the police. But where are the taillights, you ask?

CHAPTER FOUR

Nasty

1933 Plymouth Coupe

Jim McClusky has owned this all-steel 1933 Plymouth five-window coupe since 1980. It was a rust bucket when he bought it, and this is the second restoration/refurbishment it's had. With this latest reincarnation, the car was endowed with a "nasty" nitrous oxide system, plenty of eye candy, and an impeccable paint job, among other refinements.

The timeless favorite engine of street rodders, a "worked" 350-ci Chevy small block powers this coupe. It is outfitted with a Competition cam, and dual quad 600 cfm Holley carburetors sit atop a polished high-rise tunnel ram manifold. A polished billet scoop feeds air to the

Classic full-fendered Mopars like this one have a look all their own. How'd you like to see this coming up fast in your rearview mirror? I know it would make me move into the right lane in a hurry.

The only part of the engine that wears paint is the block itself. As you can see here, everything else is polished billet, stainless, or chrome, including all of the hoses and plumbing for the dual-bank nitrous boost system.

hungry carbs, and everything else on the engine is polished aluminum, stainless, or chrome. The engine block is even painted to match the color of the car, and the firewall is stainless, polished to a mirror-like shine. All of the engine plumbing—and there's lots of it due to the nitrous system—is stainless braided hosing or chrome-plated hard lines.

Nitrous Oxide (N₂O)— Also simply called nitrous, nitrous oxide is commonly known as laughing gas. Nitrous is often used in drag racing to boost engine performance for short periods. When burned, N_2O releases nitrogen and oxygen; the released oxygen permits more gasoline to be burned, resulting in the boost in power.

Dual Quad— This is an engine equipped with two four-barrel carburetors.

Although the motor puts out about 475 horsepower, Jim didn't feel that was enough, so he installed a Pro Shot Fogger nitrous oxide boost system that provides an additional 350 horsepower. With the nitrous boost turned on, we're talking in excess of 800 horsepower here.

Engine cooling is handled by a Walker aluminum radiator with a polished, billet-aluminum overflow tank. The engine uses a serpentine belt setup with polished pulleys and idlers. The rearview mirror and dual door-mounted mirrors are also made of polished billet aluminum.

The rumble seat is opened and closed electrically, and it provides access for storage behind the front seats in addition to carrying a couple of passengers.

Apparently, Jim really gets into bright work, since the car's undercarriage is all polished aluminum, chrome, and stainless. A fully chromed Jaguar IRS setup is used with coil-over shocks. The rear-end gear ratio is 4.11:1.

Coil-Overs—A type of shock absorber that has an external coil spring mounted to it; coil-over shocks are usually adjustable to raise or lower ride height.

The paint is three-stage (base, color, and clear) Candy Violet from House of Kolor. Jim shot the car himself in his garage, a real testament to his prowess with a spray gun.

The interior features a polished rosewood dash and a combination heater/air conditioning system by Vintage Air. A Pioneer AM/FM/CD stereo system with a graphic equalizer pumps the tunes through six

The A/C vents and the digital GemStar gauge cluster are nestled in the beautiful rosewood dash. The panel below it holds the Pioneer stereo system, the Vintage Air heat and A/C controls, and the illuminated rocker switches that control the wipers, dash lights, electric radiator fan, and dual-bank nitrous system.

The needlework on the car's upholstery is beautiful and the custom-embroidered "Mayflower" ship insignias adorn the headrests. Everything about this car is top drawer all the way.

The laughing gas is securely stowed behind the driver's seat and held with floor-mounted clamps. All Jim has to do is reach back with his left hand to open the valve, and things start to happen in a hurry when he flips the dash mounted rocker switches to engage the boost. The nitrous system adds another 350 horsepower to a mill that's already pumping out 475 to begin with.

With the popularity of automatic transmissions, you don't see too many street rods with manual transmissions and four-on-the-floor shifters like this Hurst unit in Jim's car. The gearbox itself is a Muncie M-21.

Although the car was neither chopped nor channeled, It has a low, clean look about it. It's a good idea to don sunglasses before taking a close look at the engine compartment—there's such a bevy of bright work there that it's almost blinding.

speakers and GemStar digital gauges give Jim feedback on the car's systems and speed. A Billet Specialties steering wheel is mounted to a cream-colored tilt steering column that's suspended by a billet hanger.

Illuminated rocker switches control the wipers, gauges, and electric fan, as well as activate the dual-bank nitrous system. There is also a button located on the switch panel for purging the nitrous system. The laughing gas bottle is secured by brackets to the floor behind the driver's seat, with the flow valve within

easy reach, although Jim confesses that he doesn't use the boost system too much.

The seats are upholstered in Naugahyde and leather. Custom-embroidered "Mayflower" ship emblems, the Plymouth insignia, are stitched on the headrests of the cream-colored seats. The coupe, which Jim nicknamed *Nasty*, also has a solenoid-operated rumble seat, doors, a remote-release gas door, and power windows.

The transmission is a four-speed manual Muncie M-21 with a Hurst shifter. The five-spoke Billet Specialties mags wear Avon ZZ1 rubber at all four corners.

CHAPTER FIVE

Little Miss Lizzy

1936 International

C-Series Stake Bed Truck

Roy Merkel spotted this radical truck on his way home from work several years back and decided he just had to have it. It's a 1936 International C-Series Street Rod that started life as a stake-bed dump truck. The body is all steel with the exception of the fiberglass Model-A fenders. The body received a healthy top chop, channeling, and raking. The truck originally came from Newfoundland, Canada. As is sometimes the case, the fellow who built the truck sold it to Roy so he could embark on another street rod project.

The truck is all steel except for the fiberglass fenders, aluminum bed, and oak rails. Polished aluminum step plates adorn the running boards, and the tilt-out windshield and original radiator shell give the truck "period" character. The bug-eye headlights and nerf bar front bumper also contribute to the retro look.

A pink prop rod keeps the louvered hood elevated for access to the power plant. A nice blend of billet and chrome is accented by the black trimmed Mickey Thompson valve covers.

Roy named the truck *Little Miss Lizzy* in honor of his daughter, Elizabeth, who immediately became his constant cruising partner, riding "shotgun" whenever he took the truck out for a spin.

A 350-ci Chevrolet engine resides under the truck's louvered hood. The engine has four-bolt main bearings, 10:1 pistons, an Edelbrock Performer manifold, a Crane 350-horse cam, and a 550 cfm Holly four-barrel carburetor. The spark comes from a Mallory Promaster coil.

The power train consists of a Chevy TH 400 transmission with a shift kit and a B&M Automotive torque converter. This couples to a narrowed 9-inch Ford positraction rear with 3.55:1 gearing, Strange axles, and All-American coil-over shocks.

The front end uses Mustang II IFS. An electric fan keeps things cool in the engine compartment. Nerf bar

bumpers are used at the front, and bug-eye headlights are mounted to the fiberglass fenders.

IFS— This is an abbreviation for Independent Front Suspension. The Ford Mustang II IFS setup is very popular and frequently used on street rods.

Nerf Bar— A custom-made bumper made of either solid or tubular stock and usually chromed.

Engine compartment eye candy consists of a chrome alternator and water pump, Mickey Thompson aluminum valve covers with extended wing nuts, a chrome air cleaner and electric fuel pump, thermostat housing, and braided stainless lines and hose covers. Billet-aluminum looms riding on anodized rails are used to route the hot pink plug

Radically chopped, channeled, and raked, the truck has a wide, squat look. While it started life out in 1936 as a stake-bed dump truck, the "Pro Streetrod" script on the grille tells it like it is today.

Because the top was chopped so radically, there isn't much visibility out the rear window. Roy got around that problem by installing a side mirror mounted on a bracket attached to the roof. The spun aluminum Moon gas tank is right at home on the aluminum 5x5 diamond plate bed.

The polished Cragar S/S mags are always in good taste and the spinner hubs add some extra pop. The truck has drum brakes on all four wheels, and the drums are painted to match the body's Candy Hot Pink color. Super Trapp mufflers give this little hauler a husky sound.

wires, and a polished Truck Stuff firewall gives the engine compartment a nice finishing touch.

Bug Eyes— These are large, round discrete headlights mounted to the fenders or a bow-bar.

The chassis was entirely hand fabricated using 2x4-inch steel tubing. The bed was hand-built from 5x5-inch aluminum diamond plate with oak bed rails. A spun-aluminum Moon gas tank resides on the bed just in back of the cab.

Powder-coated block-hugger headers mate up with Super Trapp mufflers at the rear of the truck, and nostalgic blue dots adorn the centers of the taillights. Polished Cragar S/S mags with knock-off hubs and Street Pro tires are used all around.

The paint is DuPont Candy Hot Pink. The distribution of electricity is handled via a Ron Francis Wiring harness. There are no exterior door handles, since the suicide doors are solenoid-operated using a wireless remote control unit. The tilt-out windshield was retained to help keep the cab cool in summer.

The diamond plate theme is carried out in the interior of *Little Miss Lizzy* as well. The floor is the same 5x5-inch aluminum diamond plate as the bed, brake, and accelerator pedals. The door panels are made of black and silver diamond-pleated Naugahyde. The tilt-steering column is outfitted with a LeCarra

The original radiator shell was retained, complete with the chrome and enamel "International" emblem.

wheel. A floor-mounted, tall, retro-look shifter with a black leather boot and an 8-ball knob engages the transmission. The gauges are VDO analog units mounted on a billet dash panel, and a large-faced bracket-mounted analog tachometer keeps tabs on the rev situation. The seats are charcoal gray cloth with darker gray leather trim, and an AM/FM/cassette stereo provides the music. The cab is also equipped with a center floor-mounted handbrake and a fire extinguisher. *Little Miss Lizzy* has manual steering but power windows.

Owing to its light weight and massive power, this little truck really hauls.

The interior is both functional and tastefully appointed. The cloth seating surfaces are cooler in the summer than leather or Naugahyde. Note the aluminum diamond plate brake pedal.

The electric radiator fan is visible through the grille here. When the 350 Chevy mill was stuffed into the cramped engine compartment, there wasn't enough clearance to run a mechanical fan driven by pulleys, so the electric unit was the way to go.

CHAPTER SIX

'22 T-Bucket
1922 Ford Model T-Bucket

"T-Buckets" get their name from the fact that the passenger compartment is shaped like a bucket. These street rods are an entity all to themselves—mostly engine with the bare minimums for everything else, including chassis and body.

It's been said that you have to be a little nuts to drive a T-Bucket, since the horsepower-to-weight ratio is wildly disproportionate, to put it politely. T-buckets are unusual, and Mike and Jackie Yencarelli's T-Bucket certainly dares to be different.

The first thing that catches your eye about this rod is that it's missing a couple of cylinders. While we're all accustomed to seeing V-8s (sometimes mammoth V-8s)

Every T-Bucket has a look of its own, and this one is no exception. Note the tubular chromed nerf bar front bumper as well as the chromed windshield supports. The rectangular headlights work well here.

If you're only counting three cylinders on this side of the engine, that's because it's a V-6. This highly unusual power plant for a street rod started out as a GM marine engine, and after the appropriate performance mods were completed, it went from boat to T-Bucket. There's lots of attention to detail in the engine department.

nestled in street rods, it is rare, indeed, to come across a V-6 as a rod power plant. This car's engine started out as a 229-ci V-6 General Motors marine engine.

T-Bucket— A highly modified Ford Model T that is usually fenderless and topless. Most T-Buckets on the road today are kit cars or replicars.

The engine was bored .060 over to bring its displacement to 292 ci, fully blueprinted and balanced, and the heads were honed and decked to give the motor an 11:1 compression ratio. Mike also used polished rods with bolts from a big-block engine to hold them together. 1.94-inch intake and 1.60-inch exhaust valves help the engine breathe easier, as do ported and polished heads with 60cc chambers. A

Crane cam, springs, and roller rockers handle the valve train chores.

Balanced— Normally used to define balancing the rotating mass (i.e., crankshaft), but this term can also mean matching the weights of the pistons and rods.

Blueprinted—Ensures the dimensions of the parts in the engine are more accurate and, therefore, closer to the original engine blueprint values.

A Victory Bow Tie intake manifold directs the fuel pumped by a 650 cfm Carter AFB four-barrel carb to the ports that are matched to the heads. To provide the spark, Mike used a GM HEI ignition upgraded with Accel parts.

Other engine goodies include a chrome oil pan and timing cover, a big block high-volume oil pump, dual remote oil filters, and braided stainless steel lines. A four-core radiator makes sure that his hot T-Bucket runs cool, and chrome Sanderson headers coupled to polished Super Trapp mufflers route the exhaust.

The transmission is the ever-popular Chevy TH-350 with a Genie shifter, a polished trans case, stock torque converter, chrome pan and dust covers, and a remote trans oil cooler.

The suspension on T-Buckets is always something to behold, and this one is no exception. It uses a Pinto front end with five-bolt rotors, chrome tubular "A" arms, and an A-1 Racing Components rack and pinion steering system.

Around the back of the rod, a narrowed 1967 Olds rear end measures a mere 30 inches from flange to flange and holds Henry axles with 3.24:1 positraction gearing. Four-link stainless steel hemi-joint suspension puts some bounce in the ride.

The replica fiberglass body is a product of Speedway Motors and it's outfitted with replica 1922 lanterns for the tail and turn signals, mounted on chrome moly brackets. A hand-operated wind-

Note how the 650 cfm Carter AFB four barrel sits catty-cornered atop the high-rise intake manifold. This configuration provides better air/fuel distribution to the six-cylinder engine. The distributor sports Accel performance mods to deliver more spark to the plugs.

The cabin of the T-Bucket is functional and comfy with the pleated Naugahyde upholstery. The gauges are Cyberdyne digital units with red LED readouts. For road music an AM/FM stereo radio with cassette provides the tunes. The seat belts are color-coordinated to match the body color, and polished billet aluminum provides some interior eye candy.

The lanterns used for the front turn signals and rear taillights/turn signals are replicas of the original 1922 Ford Model T lanterns. They're mounted to the rod with custom chrome moly brackets.

A huge Mr. Roadster polished aluminum air cleaner keeps dust, bugs, and other foreign matter from getting into the engine via the carburetor, and it looks cool, too.

In this rear shot you can see the lantern tail lamps nestled within the tubular nerf bar rear bumper. While the body is fiberglass, the fenders were formed of sheet metal to cover the humongous Mickey Thompson rear tires.

shield wiper on the driver's side is a novel touch on what can rightly be called a totally impractical car.

Inside the "bucket" itself are a polished billet steering column and go and stop pedals, and Cyberdyne red LED digital read-out gauges. The seats and door panels are upholstered in tan tuck and pleated Naugahyde. In true roadster tradition, there are no side windows or exterior door handles. And this T-Bucket doesn't even have a convertible top,

making the incongruity of the single manual windshield wiper even more outrageous.

The rod's running gear consists of 15x5-inch polished-aluminum Weld Racing wheels with 165SR15 Road Handlers; the rears are 15x14-inch aluminum CC Racing wheels wearing monster 29X1850 Mickey Thompson tires.

Like I said earlier, this is one T-Bucket that dares to be different.

CHAPTER SEVEN

A Visit to Posies Rods & Customs

Ken Fenical was a young, itinerant pinstriper who had a love for automobiles and all things mechanical. His skills were honed from a hands-on approach, and he built his first street rod, a Ford Model A panel delivery truck, while in his teens. Since this truck was Ken's everyday transportation, his dad took advantage of the signage opportunities it presented and had the name "Posies" painted on the sides of the truck to help advertise the family's florist business. Ken adopted the name and hung out a shingle to announce the opening of his first shop

This bad Model A is a customer's car that came all the way to Pennsylvania from Georgia. Posies' clients hail from all over the country.

The shop is always full of customer project vehicles. Posies has enjoyed a steady stream of business from the first day Ken hung the shingle out in 1964.

in 1964. He and his employees have been building street rods and customs and making and selling parts ever since.

Ken has made his living building street rods and customs and modifying vehicles from the first day he opened his shop. When asked about the success of his business, he simply says, "Nobody ever told me I couldn't make a living at it, so I guess I never gave that a thought. I've been busy since day one."

One of Ken's more remarkable creations is his *Extremeliner*. Inspired by the French Hispano-Suiza motorcar of the 1920s and the 1930s and the traditional surfer's woody station wagon, Ken set out to create a truly one-of-a-kind vehicle.

Woody— A woody is a vehicle that incorporates natural finished wood for structure of exposed body panels, such as the station wagons from the 1930s and 1940s that were frequently used by surfers to transport their surfboards.

The *Extremeliner* is an entirely hand-built vehicle. Posies based the design on the Hispano-Suiza crossed with a "woody," and this is the awesome result.

The *Extremeliner* is now available as a 1:24 scale die cast model from Ertl, and the *Orange Krisp* custom station wagon on the shelf here, as well as some of the other Posies creations, are also available as models.

All of the Posies employees are master craftsmen in their own right. Here an old truck is getting some metal work massaged. The steel running boards on the truck were handmade in the shop.

"Creation" is indeed the right word to use here, as this vehicle was entirely handmade—everything except the tires, axles, wheel bearings, transmission, and engine was hand-fabricated right in the Posies shop. Unlike other customs that are based on a production chassis and sheet metal from an existing car, the *Extremeliner* was built from the ground up, literally.

When I first saw the *Extremeliner*, I commented on how great the car's woodwork looked. Needless to say, I was extremely surprised when Ken told me that it was not wood, but steel painted to look like wood. Even on extremely close examination I found it hard to believe that this was a paint job—the detailing was incredible, right down to the occasional knot in the graining.

Ken has exhibited the car at shows across the nation, and Ertl made a die-cast model of the car in

1:24th scale. Several other Posies' creations have also been immortalized as models. A tour of the Posies' facility is something every motorhead would enjoy. In addition to a full paint shop, there are such exotic tools as English wheels, planishing hammers, metal bending brakes, all sorts of chop saws and presses, oxyacetylene, arc, MIG, and TIG welders, and plasma cutters. In short, everything you'd need to build a car from scratch.

As you would expect, Ken employs highly skilled craftsmen, and the capabilities list for his shop includes metal shaping, machine shop services, glass cutting and edging, louvering services in three different sizes, and sheet metal restoration. Posies also produces custom-made bucks for hand-formed sheet metal, and they perform tube bending for exhaust systems and roll cages. Plus, the Posies staff provides electrical wiring and stainless steel restoration and construction. Kind of a one-stop super shop, you might say.

Without a doubt, Posies is probably best known for its Super Slide springs. Ken realized long ago that the original springs on the early rods were tired, weak, and just plain unsafe, so he began building springs that would allow a car to sit low while still delivering good ride quality—he also devised a way to reduce the friction that leaf springs produce. He called his improved springs "Super Slide." These springs feature a nylon button between the leaves that permits the leaves to move with less friction, which produces a better ride and extends the life of the spring. Many of Posies' Super Slide customers have over 100,000 miles on their street rods, which is a testament to how well the springs work.

Posies did a 1957 Chevy custom for Vic Edelbrock of carburetor and intake manifold fame, and the shop has a number of other high-profile clients. ZZ Top guitarist and car enthusiast Billy Gibbons stops in to say "hello" to Ken and his crew whenever he's in the area.

The shop is located in the quiet burg of Hummelstown, Pennsylvania, and if you're ever in the area, stop in and pay the Posies team a visit. It is definitely a worthwhile experience I'm sure you'll enjoy.

Be sure to check out the *Cookie Cutter* (chapter 9) to see what Ken's personal '32 Deuce roadster looks like.

Posies stocks, sells, and ships custom street rod parts and their own Super Slider springs all over the world. If you need a part, chances are good that Posies has it in stock or can get it for you, pronto.

This Model A's engine is as clean and impressive as the rest of the car. A Corvette LT4 injected 350 helps it to haul without breathing hard.

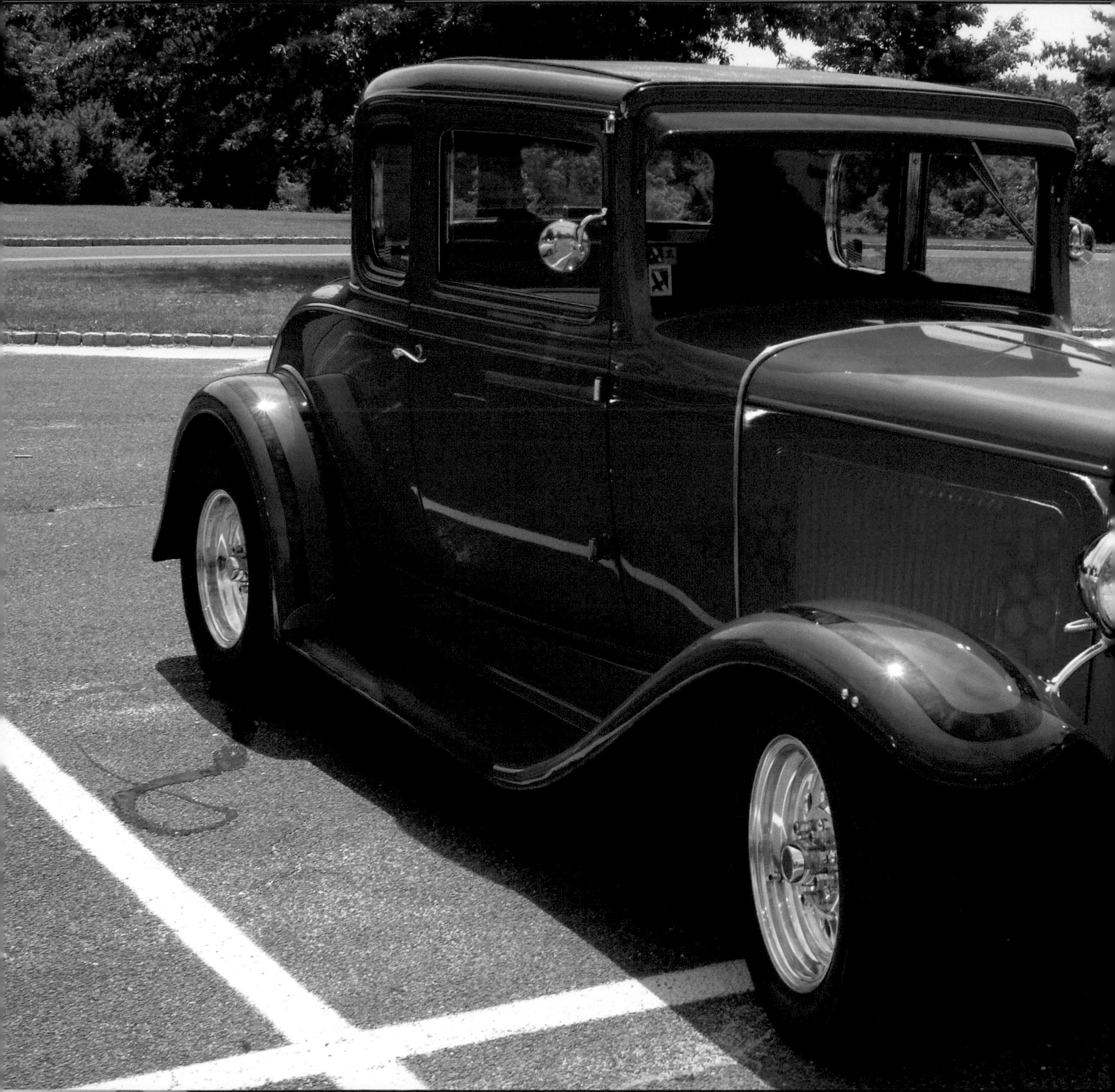

CHAPTER EIGHT

Tangerine Dream

1931 Chevrolet Bowtie Coupe

There's something about a street rod that catches your eye and grabs your attention, regardless of what year, make, or model the rod is. In the case of Baron and Marion Yeager's 1931 Chevy coupe, it's the candy tangerine-orange color and the incredible painting effects that say, "Hey, look at me!" But before we talk about the exterior of this rod, let's take a peek under the hood.

The venerable small-block 350 Chevrolet engine is bored .030 over and has been enhanced with a street cam to give it some extra punch without being too radical. For carburetion, an AFB 650 cfm four-barrel supplies the go-juice. The power is transmitted through a Chevy

Michelin rubber on the front and Goodyears on the rear give *Tangerine Dream* good traction and handling. The radiator shell and grille are from a '32 Ford, and it causes some confusion to folks who are trying to figure out what make the car is. Virtually every other component is Chevrolet or aftermarket.

Plenty of chrome eye candy resides under *Tangerine Dream's* engine hood, and the plug wires are orange, naturally.

TH700R4 transmission which, in turn, passes it on to the Dana 60 posi rear running 3.35:1 gears.

Since this car originally had a straight six motor when it rolled off the assembly line in 1931, stuffing a 350 into the narrow nose of the car required some "imagineering." Block hugger headers were used to route the exhaust gases through Monza mufflers with dual tips. The alternator, which is usually mounted topside on an engine, was relocated to the left side below the headers to get it out of the way. A tasteful amount of chrome, including chrome radiator hoses, valve covers, air cleaner, pulleys, wing nuts, and alternator give the engine compartment some sparkle, topped off with orange spark-plug wires to keep the "tangerine" theme consistent.

The front suspension is the popular Mustang II IFS setup, while the rear suspension utilizes leaf springs to support the Dana 60 rear. Aluminum

wheels by Weld are used all around with Michelins on the front and Goodyears on the rear.

Flush-mounted LED lights signal turns and braking at the rear, augmented by a bow tie-shaped "cyclops" brake light in the rear window. The front lights are chromed units with the vintage look, mounted on a chrome bow that spans from one fender to the other.

A LeCarra steering wheel with a bow tie horn button is mounted on the tilt column, and VDO analog gauges mounted in a genuine walnut dash keep Baron up to speed on what's going on under the hood. Air conditioning is by Rainbow Air, and an AM/FM stereo with CD player provides the cruising music. Gear selection for the automatic transmission is accomplished with a floor-mounted Genie shifter.

To keep the resto rod look, the soft top was retained. The rest of the car is steel, including the

With space in the engine compartment at a premium, block hugger headers were a must, as was relocating the alternator lower down on the engine below the headers.

fenders and running boards—something you don't see too much of these days.

Resto Rod— An original-looking car with a modified chassis, power plant, or drivetrain.

Most folks aren't sure what make the car is when they first see it, and this is compounded by the use of a 1932 Ford radiator shell and grill instead of the stock 1931 Chevy unit. The Deuce nose helps to keep the car's lines smooth while preserving the resto rod look.

Deuce— This is a nickname for a 1932 Ford coupe or roadster.

The paint on *Tangerine Dream* is, in a word, amazing. The rich candy tangerine orange is a three-stage paint job consisting of a reflective base coat, a transparent color coat, and then clear coat on top. But wait—there's more! Over the clear coat some "bubble scalloping" (for lack of a better description) was applied. Virtually everyone who sees this effect marvels at its intricacy, but they don't have a clue how it was achieved, and neither did I until Baron let me in on the secret.

For the front and rear fender bubble scalloping, the areas were first masked off. Then, using a lit oxyacetylene torch with the oxygen turned off, the acetylene was jetted onto the unmasked areas, using

Dual-tipped Monza mufflers let the spent gas exit the rear of the car with class, and the flush-mounted LED tail lights/turn signals let anyone following know Baron's intentions. The bow tie-shaped "cyclops" upper brake light further enforces the signal to "whoa."

putty knives and metal discs to dodge the carbon-rich smoke to create the various patterns. Who woulda thunk it?

The almost-ghosted "bubbles" on the sides of the engine hood in front of and behind the side louvers was done in the same manner, but from a greater distance, to make the carbon patterns lighter. No matter how you slice it, only a very steady hand and an enormous amount of skill can achieve these effects. When all of the effects were applied, several coats of clear coat were sprayed on to preserve and protect them.

As if that wasn't enough, an airbrushed mural of the car in the foreground and mountains in the background was applied to the trunk. Yup, the car says, "Hey, look at me," big-time.

This airbrushed mural adorns the trunk of *Tangerine Dream* and, like all the other paint on the car, grabs and holds the attention of anyone who sees it.

The door panels and headliner are pleated black Naugahyde, and the hand-crafted dash is made of walnut. VDO analog gauges, a matte-black LeCarra steering wheel trimmed in black leather, and a bow tie horn button make the interior cozy and functional. A/C and a great stereo system both contribute to comfortable cruising.

Here you can see the "ghost bubbles" that adorn the sides of the engine hood and carry over onto the front edges of the doors. The paint isn't just spectacular, it's flawless.

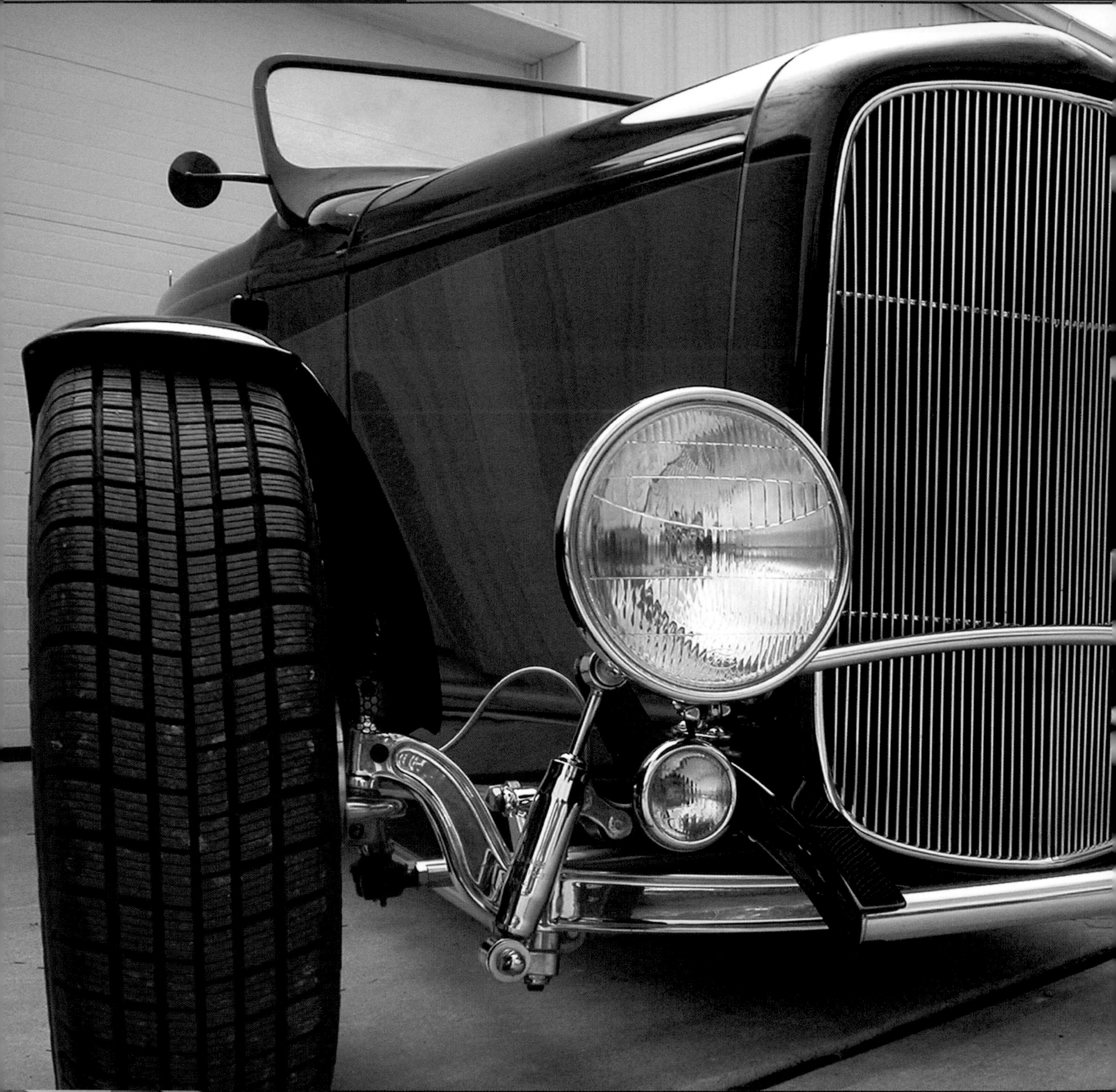

CHAPTER NINE

Cookie Cutter

1932 Ford Deuce Roadster

What kind of street rod would you build if you were a master craftsman and had all the resources and equipment of a professional rod shop at your disposal? I'll bet that's a hard one for you to answer, because it certainly is for me. Fortunately for Ken Fenical, it was a no-brainer. Ken decided to build the quintessential American street rod: a 1932 Ford Deuce roadster that he dubbed *Cookie Cutter*.

Ken started out with a frame from Curbside Hot Rod Parts, who kicked it up at the fire wall by bringing the front cross member up 2 inches. Walker Radiators made a 2-inch-shorter radiator to accommodate the modified cross member. The

The *Cookie Cutter* was built intentionally to be reminiscent of the way street rods used to be built. Touches like the large headlights and the dropped I-beam front axle evoke memories of the rodding trends a few decades back. The nostalgia trend is making a big-time comeback, and this rod fits it like a hand in a glove.

You'll notice that there are no outside door handles on the car and, unlike most other shaved rods, Ken doesn't have solenoid-activated poppers on the doors either. In true roadster tradition, the *Cookie Cutter* has no windows, so opening the doors is accomplished by reaching in and using the inside door handles.

idea behind this was to give the car a strong rake, and it worked out fine.

Roadster— A convertible without side windows; sometimes they don't even have tops.

He dropped an all-steel Brookville Roadster body on the frame and fashioned the four cycle fenders in the Posies shop using an English wheel and a Pullmax

(fenders are required on all vehicles in Pennsylvania, even street rods). Ken also converted '32 Ford cowl lights for the taillights, whereas the headlights are '33 commercial units that he downsized in depth.

Ken used a So-Cal Speed Shop windshield frame that he powder-coated in black. He also fabricated the longer hood from .080 aluminum.

Unlike a lot of street rodders who use small-block Chevy mills in their rods, Ken decided to keep his

The subtle bronze-colored accent panel is visible in this elevated shot of the car's left side. House of Kolor base coat and clear coat were used for both the black and bronze colors.

Ford all Ford. For power, he chose a cast-iron 302-ci engine that puts out a conservative 200 horsepower, feeding it with a 500 cfm Edelbrock carb.

The rest of the power train consists of an automatic C4 gearbox from Del Transmissions, coupled to an 8-inch Ford rear end with 3.70 gears.

For running gear, the *Cookie Cutter* wears Colorado Custom "Grizzly" wheels all around, with 16-inchers in the front and 18-inchers at the rear. The tires are Michelin.

The interior is tan leather and the seat comes from Tea's Designs, while the gauges are Hane-

The cycle fenders on all four wheels, required by law in Pennsylvania, were hand-fabricated by Ken in his shop using an English wheel.

The steering wheel from Colorado Custom matches the wheels on the car. Map pockets sewn into the leather door panels provide storage in the absence of a glove box.

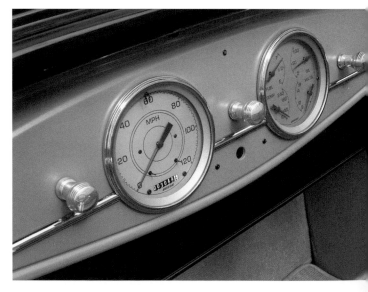

Haneline gauges give the dash a real retro look, which is "in" these days.

Here's a view of the car you don't get to see often—the convertible top is up! Check out the gorgeous Colorado Custom wheels—18 inches on the rear and 16 inches on the front.

line units. To keep things comfy in the cabin, a Vintage Air A/C and heat system was installed, and a Colorado Custom steering wheel connected to a billet column points the rod in the desired direction.

The paint is black and bronze base coat and clear coat from the House of Kolor.

As this book was going to press, Ken sold the *Cookie Cutter* and started working on another rod that he says will eclipse or surpass this beautiful black Deuce roadster. After seeing this rod in person, there's no reason for me to doubt him.

Shaved— Door handles and body trim that have been removed and smoothed over.

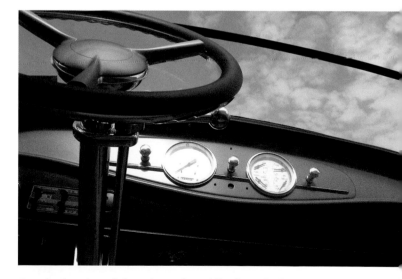

Herein lies the real appeal of a roadster—plenty of blue sky overhead to cruise under.

CHAPTER TEN

Screaming Mimi

1933 Dodge 5-Window Coupe

I'm a pretty fortunate guy to have a wife who is almost as much of a car nut as I am. In fact, she's the one who spotted *Screaming Mimi* while we were spending the Memorial Day Weekend in Cape Cod about a decade ago. Before the weekend was over, we bought this wild little coupe for her.

The fellow we bought the car from was the owner of a garage and had built the car to go in a straight line for a quarter of a mile at a time; in other words, the car was built for the drag strip rather than casual cruising on the streets. Owing to that fact, there was a bit of work that had to be done to make it "streetable." Little things, like

The big block mill, high-rise butterfly scoop, flamed paint job, and headers with baloney-slashed mufflers make *Screaming Mimi* look like it's going fast even when it's standing still. This car gets lots of "thumbs-up" and "OK" signs from folks who see it—even from the police.

The car has plenty of attitude and gobs of power. The front turn signals came from a 1978 Harley-Davidson Superglide, one of many innovations I used on this rod.

adding turn signals, a horn, brake lights, functional headlights, and other details that would surely earn us a summons if they weren't taken care of. But that was actually a good thing, since I got to know the car intimately by working on it.

Liz and I named the car *Screaming Mimi* after an expression that my mom used occasionally. It certainly seemed to fit the car's attitude and disposition.

Mimi's power plant is a big block Chevy motor that came from a 1972 Monte Carlo. It has 402 ci, 11:1 domed pistons, a Mallory dual point distrib-utor, MSD ignition, a 10-degree cam, dual 500 cfm Edelbrock four-barrel carbs on a high-rise aluminum Edelbrock Tunnel Ram manifold, and four-bolt mains. The motor was balanced and blue-printed and rated at 500-plus horsepower on the dyno. *Screaming Mimi* is certainly not at a loss for go-power.

The transmission is a Chevrolet Turbo Hydramatic 350 with a 1,600-rpm stall speed converter. A B&M Automotive Z-Gate Ratchet shift kit with a T-handle shifter selects gears.

The transverse leaf spring and independent suspension came from a 1969 Corvette. Gearing is 3.71:1 and individually adjustable air shocks adjust the ride height and harshness or softness.

The rear end came from a 1969 Corvette and has independent suspension, individually adjustable air shocks, 3.71:1 posi-traction gearing, and Corvette disc brakes.

The body, trunk lid, and chassis are all steel and started out as a production 1933 Dodge five-window coupe. The roof and front vent were filled in and it has a fiberglass 1932 Ford radiator shell with a '33 Dodge ram-head radiator ornament mounted on it. The paint on the body and chassis is Chrysler Black Cherry base coat and clear coat; Chrysler Firestorm acrylic lacquer was used for the flames and front-end components. The body is channeled and molded to the frame, which also has extensive molding.

Molded— Body and/or chassis seams that have been filled in or otherwise smoothed out.

The upholstery is red and black pleated panel Naugahyde, and the trunk and 16-gallon fuel cell mounted in the trunk are also upholstered to match. Five-point racing harnesses attach to the competition bucket seats, and dark smoke-tinted glass adorns the side and rear windows. A Sony 100-watt AM/FM/cassette stereo hides in the overhead console with 7-inch round Sony speakers mounted behind the seats.

A leather-wrapped Grant steering wheel with polished aluminum spokes mates to a nontilting Ford steering column. The ignition key in the column locks the wheel so the car can't be steered, but it has nothing to do with the ignition. That's handled by the rocker switches below the gauge cluster, and they have to be turned on in a special sequence to avoid getting a nasty zap—a little crude-and-rude theft prevention measure I rigged up.

The five-point racing harnesses on the competition bucket seats give the message that this car can really haul.

The inside illumination comes from overhead-mounted aviation-style lights. There's also a "chaser" cyclops L.E.D. brake/turn signal light, and "firefly" L.E.D. valve stem lights give the wheels a cool red glow when they are spinning.

The instrumentation consists of a Cyberdine red LCD digital dash with zero to 60 miles-per-hour timer. The gauges include a digital tach, digital zero to 200 miles-per-hour speedo, digital fuel, oil pressure, and temperature gauges. We installed a competition rocker switch panel and all-solid state sensors and sending units as well.

The front end uses a solid I-beam dropped 1961 Ford van axle with manual rack and pinion steering. The binders up front are manual drum

The 100-watt Sony AM/FM/cassette stereo is housed in the overhead console. Note the mini rearview mirror mounted next to the stereo. The door panels, seats, headliner, console, trunk, and fuel cell cover are all upholstered with pleated panel black and red Naugahyde.

brakes with a front drum/rear disk proportioning valve located under the dashboard.

Binders— This is a slang term for brakes.

Weighing in at just under 1,700 pounds, the car is immensely overpowered, and it's easy to burn rubber and even pop wheelies with street tires. It rides and handles like a big go-cart on steroids. And when people see Liz behind the wheel, they do a double take. The car brings smiles to people's faces when they see it—after all, it isn't every day you see a full-size "Hot Wheels" car on the road.

A vintage metal "aah-ooga" horn handles the warning chores with a real nostalgia sound. The solid dropped I-beam front axle came from a '61 Ford van.

The Dodge Ram ornament mounted on the '32 Ford radiator shell tells you this is no Deuce. The butterfly scoop in back of it helps to feed copious amounts of air to the twin 500 cfm four-barrel carbs mounted on the high-rise tunnel ram manifold.

CHAPTER ELEVEN

Gary's '37 Cabriolet

1937 Ford Cabriolet

Gary Van Wagner set out in search of a street rod that would stand out in a crowd. His search came to an end when he happened upon a 1937 Ford Cabriolet built by Gibbons of Darlington, NC. This car was a prototype rod for Gibbons and was built from the ground up using the original 1937 Ford chassis as its foundation. While '37 Ford Coupes are perennial favorites for building street rods, it's rare to find a '37 cabriolet, especially one so well executed.

The car is exceptionally sleek and smooth, thanks to a thin coating of fiberglass over the all-steel body to soften the harsh edges and make the curves more

Although you see lots of 1937 Ford coupe street rods, Cabriolets are a rarity, for sure. Gary's Cabriolet is an excellent example of a street rod done right.

Like the exterior of the car, the dash is clean and uncluttered as well. Red fluorescent Dakota Digital instrumentation is centered on the dash, with the outlets for the Vintage Air at either side. A four-spoke LeCarra billet steering wheel wrapped in blue leather matches the blue English wool and leather-trimmed seats. Billet pedals and a billet rearview mirror are the perfect finishing touches. Gary has a CB radio mounted under the dash.

sinewy. The car has 11 coats of 1980 Corvette White with some PPG pearl mixed in to endow it with iridescence. Seven coats of clear on top of the color coats produce an incredible luster. In bright sunlight, the car is almost blinding. Fine hand-painted, two-tone accent striping runs along the beltline for the full length of the car, keeping the blue-on-white theme consistent.

Interior appointments include blue English wool and leather seat upholstery with navy blue Mercedes wool pile carpeting. Red fluorescent Dakota Digital instruments accent the dash, and billet-aluminum

pedals, levers, and handles further complement the passenger compartment.

The tilt-telescopic steering column, originally from a 1978 Chevrolet van, is suspended from a billet hanger with a LeCarra four-spoke billet steering wheel covered in padded navy leather mounted to it.

Creature comforts include power windows, power locks, a power rumble seat, and air conditioning and heat by Vintage Air. Cruising sounds come from a 200-watt Panasonic stereo AM/FM/cassette and CD changer equipped with a graphic equalizer, mounted in the rear

A 350ci Corvette LT1 engine provides the ponies to get this Cabriolet moving. Blue accents, plug wires, and accessories give the engine compartment some extra eye candy, too.

bulkhead in front of the rumble seat. The main rear speakers are also mounted on this bulkhead, and there's plenty of bass to be had by adjusting the equalizer bands.

Rumble Seat— An open, fold-up rear seat located where the trunk would normally be.

The blue-on-white theme is carried right into the engine compartment where a 1970 350-ci Corvette LT1 engine lurks under the hood. The 350-horsepower output of the engine is transferred to the rear wheels through a bone-stock Chevy TH350 trans and stock torque converter that couples to an 8.8-inch Ford rear. With a rear end sporting 3:00 gears, Gary boasts that the car gets 17.5 miles to the gallon, and he says, "It drives like a dream—it's extremely

comfortable and utterly reliable." Understandably, he enjoys getting the "thumbs-up" and "OK" signs from other motorists, pedestrians, and fellow rodders.

The rolling stock consists of vintage one-piece American Racing Torq Thrust II wheels (the current Torq Thrusts are two-piece wheels) riding on Michelin radials all around. Stopping power comes from front discs and rear drums.

Teardrops— Headlights that are round at the top and taper smoothly to a point at the bottom, resembling a tear drop. The stock 1937 Ford headlights are teardrops, for example.

The Chrysler torsion bar front suspension is a very unique touch, and something you don't see too often

Between the reflections of the brilliant white paint with a generous dose of pearl added for good measure and the highly polished mags, Gary's Cabriolet is almost blinding when viewed in bright sunlight.

in a world dominated by Mustang II IFS systems and dropped I-beam or tube front axles. The torsion bar system allows the ride height of the car to be easily adjusted to give it more or less rake, as desired.

The removable Carson top was built by Gibbons and then shipped to Carson in Kansas. Carson installed the English wool headliner and the navy blue canvas covering and then shipped it back to Gibbons where it was mounted on the car. As is the case with all true cabriolets, there is no soft folding top like the one that convertibles are equipped with. So if there's even a remote possibility of rain, Gary drives his cabriolet with the Carson top in place—better to be safe than sorry.

Carson Top— A solid, removable roof that is covered with a soft material, named for the manufacturer in Kansas.

Smooth is the order of the day, and this rear view of the car shows it best. The all-steel body is under a thin veneer of fiberglass that softens the harshness of the steel lines and serves to give the car a molded appearance, even though all of the body components are discrete.

The classic 1937 Ford teardrop headlights were retained to keep the car's resto rod look, and the grille is stock as well. There's just enough chrome and bright work on the car to give it some pizzazz without detracting attention from the smooth lines of the body.

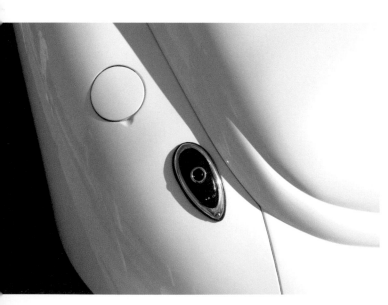

For those of you who believe every true street rod has to have blue-dot taillights to be authentic, the proof is in the pudding here. Note the smooth transition of the body as it meets the rear valance panel and the unobtrusive fuel filler door.

Here's a profile of the car with the Carson top removed and the electrically controlled rumble seat open. The Torq Thrust II mags wearing Michelin radials all around give the car a clean, uncluttered look in classic good taste.

CHAPTER TWELVE

Understated Elegance

1933 Plymouth Two-Door Sedan

Tony Castaldo has been a gear head all his life and his love of cars is evident when you take a close look at his 1933 Plymouth two-door sedan dubbed *Understated Elegance.*

Tony used a small-block Chevy engine to power the rod but, instead of going with the popular 350-ci bow tie mill, he opted instead for a vintage 1966 327-ci Chevy motor with a mild street cam. To give the engine compartment some additional dazzle, he added polished aluminum valve covers with engraved flames and installed a polished stainless steel firewall. These items are augmented with powder-coated

Though the fenders and running boards are glass, the rest of the car is vintage steel. The radiator shell was decked of its emblems to keep the "smoothy" look consistent. Period bug-eye headlights keep the resto look working.

The underhood eye candy includes these sharp billet valve covers with engraved flames, a stainless Borgeson steering joint, and powder-coated block hugger headers, among other items. The detachable hood sides allow spectators to take in the engine detailing.

block hugger headers and a polished stainless steel Borgeson knuckle. The sides of the engine hood are detachable so folks can get a good look at the engine from both sides of the car. The mill is coupled to a bone-stock Chevrolet TH400 automatic transmission that retains the original torque converter and has no shift kit installed.

Knuckle— This refers to the steering knuckle, a universal joint that connects the steering column to the steering box. Polished or chromed knuckles made by Borgeson are frequently used on street rods.

Fuel is fed via a mechanical fuel pump to the single Holley 750 cfm dual pumper four-barrel carb mounted on an aluminum Edelbrock manifold. In a world dominated by high-tech electronic devices, it's nice to see a rod that uses "old school" mechanical technology.

When viewing the car from the rear, you can really appreciate its symmetry and clean lines. The radio antenna is a short black whip unit mounted directly above the rear window.

The cream-colored, leather-rimmed LeCarra wheel is mounted on a painted Ididit column and hanger, while Classic gauges rimmed with gold bezels populate the center of the dash. Two-tone saddle and desert tan leather is used for the upholstery on the door panels, seats, and headliner.

Gold-anodized billet aluminum components like the horn button and the gear shift lever, as well as the door handles and window cranks, keep the theme consistent with the gold bezel gauges. The color LCD monitor displays the output from the rear-window-mounted color video camera to keep the driver posted on what's happening behind the vehicle.

Coil-over adjustable shocks are used on the front, coupled to the popular Mustang II IFS. Around back, the rear is a Ford 9-inch banjo with 3.50:1 gearing, suspended by leaf springs and tempered by coil-overs. The exhaust system is a Castaldo-made custom design outfitted with small glass-pack mufflers to give the exhaust notes some tone.

Glass-Packs— Loud, aftermarket mufflers that are packed with fiberglass instead of the steel baffles used in stock mufflers.

The rod relies on "armstrong power" for the steering, brakes, and windows, all of which are manual. Tony plans on adding these improvements, along with air conditioning, as the budget permits (he's working on another rod project, so the equitable distribution of funds between the two cars is a fine balancing act).

In the interior, the all-steel dash uses Classic gauges with gold bezels. Other aluminum parts such as the door handles and the column-mounted shift lever are gold anodized to keep the metal trim consistent. The interior upholstery is finished in saddle and desert sand two-tone leather, and a LeCarra leather-wrapped steering wheel is mounted on an Ididit steering column, painted to match the car.

An upholstered overhead console houses the AM/FM/CD stereo system with a graphic equalizer as well as the switches for the lights and other accessories. A color digital video camera replaces the rearview mirror, as visibility is severely limited thanks to the radical 4.5-inch top chop the car underwent. A color LCD monitor mounted under the dash allows Tony to see what's going on behind the car.

The body is all steel except for the fiberglass fenders and is virtually devoid of chrome except for the two door handles, the gas cap, and the wiper-blade arm. Tony wanted the car to have a clean, uncluttered look, which he achieved.

American Racing Torq Thrust II mags outfitted with 14-inch front tires and 15-inch rears, both by

When faced front-on, all '30s Mopars have a formidable look; the painted grille and absence of front bumpers make this '33 Plymouth look even more menacing. Tony wanted to keep the chrome- and dazzle-work to a minimum in an effort to keep the lines clean and simple. Suffice it to say, it worked.

B.F. Goodrich, give the car a smart rake while maintaining the classic look.

To say the car is clean and smooth is an understatement. In fact, the name he chose to give the car, *Understated Elegance*, sums it all up very nicely. Tony enjoys driving the car frequently, and he's taken it all the way to Kentucky from New Jersey for the Street Rod Nationals.

The car's moniker is painted in script underneath the rear window. Because of the radical top chop, the rear window is barely able to provide a home to the "cyclops" brake light; a color video camera mounted to the right of the cyclops keeps Tony informed of rear-end activity.

CHAPTER THIRTEEN

'32 Highboy
1932 Ford Deuce Roadster

Denny Buckley knows what he likes, and he likes a street rod with plenty of power. That's why he opted to put a 454-ci Chevy big block motor in his '32 Ford highboy roadster. But this rod isn't all brawn; indeed, it has plenty of beauty to boot.

The scallop paint job is a stunning blend of GM Pearl White and Viper Red, and that theme is carried through on the interior as well, with red and white upholstery made of marine vinyl for weather resistance. And that's a good thing, since this highboy doesn't have a top, or side windows for that matter.

A Chevrolet Turbo Hydramatic 350 transmission with a 2,600-rpm stall converter transmits the power from the engine to the Ford 9-inch posi-traction rear

The rumble seat, seen open here, is functional and electrically operated. Two speakers for the stereo system are also mounted in the rumble seat compartment.

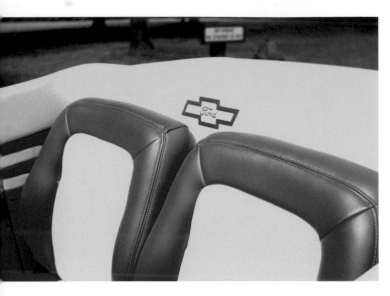

The interior color scheme matches the exterior perfectly, right down to the scalloping. Red and white marine vinyl was used for the upholstery for its weather resistance—just in case Denny gets caught in a shower (that happened the day we did this photo shoot).

The interior is clean and uncluttered, and the chrome-bezel Dolphin gauges work well here. A Pioneer AM/FM/CD player is mounted under the dash and a full-width package tray located there, too, provides storage space.

There's something intrinsically appealing about a big block Chevy engine, and this 454ci Tonawanda mill has plenty of appeal. When Denny is asked how much horsepower it cranks out, he answers simply, "Lots."

end. The gearing is 3.50:1, and a Lokar shifter engages the desired gear.

Highboy— Customized Model A or Deuce Ford that sits at stock height.

The Tonawanda crate engine has had the Buckley touch applied to it in the form of a mild RV cam, Sanderson headers, and a 750 cfm Edelbrock carburetor on an aluminum intake manifold. The appropriate eye candy is also represented by the chrome alternator, radiator hoses, brackets, and other goodies. A GM HEI distributor supplies the spark.

Crate Engine— A factory-built, ready-to-run engine that is shipped in a wooden packing crate.

An electrically operated rumble seat houses the two rear speakers of the Pioneer AM/FM/CD stereo system. The dash features analog gauges from Dolphin, and a LeCarra steering wheel mounted to an Ididit painted column suspended from a billet-aluminum hanger completes the interior appointments. Denny had the Ford script and bow tie logo

The Coca-Cola trailer is a novel touch, and it's practical, too. Denny packs his gear in it when going to distant street rod meets and there's still plenty of room left for a six-pack of brewskies.

stitched into the upholstery between the twin bucket seats.

The frame is a box unit using 1932 frame rails. The front end is a dropped I-beam solid front axle suspended by a Super Slide leaf spring from Posies. Four-bar coil-over shocks handle the rear suspension. Disc brakes on all four wheels provide the stopping power.

In true roadster fashion, because there are no side windows, there are no exterior door handles either; entering the car is done by reaching in and using the inside door handles. Wind "wings" on both sides of the

The binders are dual-piston discs on all four wheels. A Posies Super Slide leaf spring lessens the harshness from bumps transmitted through the I-beam front axle.

windshield help to deflect the breeze and keep wind noise down while cruising along at highway speeds.

Denny chose the ever-popular five-spoke Torq Thrust II wheels for the car and its accessory trailer. The trailer itself was made from an old Coca-Cola refrigerator box. Buckley welded up a nice little platform for the box to sit on and then added two matching stools. The trailer elicits memories of hanging out in the malt shop back in high school days, and the 1932 Ford gooseneck taillights on the trailer keep the nostalgia thing working.

Buckley has been a street rodder for decades, and he really gets into driving his highboy. He's taken it considerable distances to NSRA national events, he's a regular at the major cruise nights in New Jersey, and when there's nothing else doing, he enjoys taking his rod out and tooling around. Way to go, Denny.

The 1932 Ford Deuce is the quintessential street rod and Buckley's has all the lines.

Glossary

Antique— This refers to a vehicle that is 25 years old or older, in stock or unmodified condition.

Appletons— Fender-mounted spotlights, named for the manufacturer.

Baby Moons— These are small chromed hubcaps that only cover the center of the wheel.

Balanced— Normally used to define balancing the rotating mass (i.e., crankshaft), but this term can also mean matching the weights of the pistons and rods.

Banjo— This is the round differential housing of a rear end.

Beltline— The line running around a car's body formed by the bottom edges of the side windows.

Binders— This is a slang term for brakes.

Blower— A supercharger.

Blown Gasser— A supercharged, gasoline-burning engine.

Blueprinted— Ensures the dimensions of the parts in the engine are more accurate and, therefore, closer to the original engine blueprint values.

Box Frame— This is a chassis frame that uses side rails connected by cross members only at the front and back. The name derives from the fact that the side rails and front and rear cross members form a rectangular box.

Bug Eyes— These are large, round discrete headlights mounted to the fenders or a bow-bar.

Bullets— These are chromed, bullet-shaped extensions used on bumpers, grilles, and wheels.

Business Coupe— A simple two-door coupe, without a rumble seat, built between the mid-1930s and the late 1940s, also referred to as a businessman's coupe.

Cam— This refers to the camshaft, a shaft in the engine which is driven by gears, belts, or chains from the crankshaft. The camshaft has a series of cams, or lobes, that open and close intake and exhaust valves as it rotates.

Carson Top— A solid, removable roof that is covered with a soft material, named for the manufacturer in Kansas.

CFM— This is an abbreviation for Cubic Feet per Minute, which is a measurement of the volume of air a carburetor can induct. The higher the CFM, the richer the air/fuel mixture, resulting in more horsepower.

Channeled— Cutting the floor so the body rests around the frame rails rather than sitting on top of the frame. This gives an overall lowered appearance.

Chopped— A hardtop car that has had its roof lowered.

CI— A measurement of the volume of an engine's cylinders in cubic inches that denotes the total volume of the engine's combustion chambers. Essentially, the larger the ci, the more horsepower the engine can produce.

Classic— A fine or unusual motorcar built between 1925 and 1948. A classic is distinguished by its fine design, high engineering standards, and superior workmanship. Only certain important automotive makes including Duesenberg, Pierce-Arrow, Cord, Packard, Hispano-Suiza, and a few others are considered "true" classics.

Coil-Overs— A type of shock absorber that has an external coil spring mounted to it; coil-over shocks are usually adjustable to raise or lower ride height.

Convertible— An open-top car with a folding roof and side windows.

Crate Engine— A factory-built, ready-to-run engine that is shipped in a wooden packing crate.

Custom— A car that is modified in visual appearance through imaginative and technical methods to create a distinctive vehicle.

Dago— A dropped front end.

Decked— Chrome details and trim removed from the trunk and smoothed over.

Deuce— This is a nickname for a 1932 Ford coupe or roadster.

Dropped— This refers to a significantly lowered vehicle.

Dual Quad— This is an engine equipped with two four-barrel carburetors.

Dutchman Panel— The metal body piece between the rear window and the trunk.

Fade-Aways— Fenders that taper back into the body.

Fat Fendered— Fords built between 1935 and 1948 that were wide and rounded in appearance.

Fender Skirts— Body panels that cover the rear wheel wells.

Flamethrowers— Devices for electronically igniting unburned exhaust gases and shooting flames out of the tailpipes.

Flathead— An L-head or side-valve engine. The most popular flathead engine was built by Ford between 1932 and 1953.

Fordor— Slang for a four-door Ford sedan.

Frame-Off Restoration— A restoration project in which the entire vehicle is completely disassembled with all parts cleaned or replaced as necessary, so that the restored car meets the original factory specifications as closely as possible.

Frame-Up Restoration— Not as detailed as a frame-off, but involves restoring the paint, chrome, interior, and mechanicals to original specifications without complete disassembly of the car.

Frenched— These are recessed headlights or taillights that are smoothed into the body panels.

Front Clip— Either the front-end sheet metal or the section of frame in front of the fire wall.

Glass-Packs— Loud, aftermarket mufflers that are packed with fiberglass instead of the steel baffles used in stock mufflers.

Headers— Fine-tuned tubular steel exhaust manifolds that are more efficient than stock cast-iron manifolds. They are usually chromed or powder-coated.

Highboy— Customized Model A or Deuce Ford that sits at stock height.

IFS— This is an abbreviation for Independent Front Suspension. The Ford Mustang II IFS setup is very popular and frequently used on street rods.

IRS— This is an abbreviation for Independent Rear Suspension. IRS setups from Corvettes and Jaguars are sometimes used on street rods rather than "solid" rear axles.

Kit Car— A reproduction of an existing automotive design, sold in various stages of production to allow for completion and customization by the builder.

Knuckle— This refers to the steering knuckle, a universal joint that connects the steering column to the steering box. Polished or chromed knuckles made by Borgeson are frequently used on street rods.

Lakepipes— Side-exit exhaust pipes located under the rocker panels with removable block-off plates.

Land Yacht— A large luxury car, usually referring to the chromed, finned, oversized vehicles of the late 1950s to early 1960s. A prime example of a land yacht is the 1959 Cadillac.

Lead sled— A lowered, late-1940s car with filled body seams, traditionally molded-in with lead. The 1949 Mercury is a favorite for a lead sled.

Lowboy— A customized Model A or Deuce Ford that has been channeled.

Lowered— A vehicle that sits lower than stock height through suspension or frame modifications.

Lowrider— A vehicle that has been lowered by a hydraulic suspension system that can bring the ride height up in order to drive it.

Louvers— Vents or slots punched in body panels. The most commonly louvered body panel is the hood, done to increase ventilation.

Matching Numbers— A restored or original vehicle in which all serial numbers (VIN, engine, body, transmission, rear end) can be researched and identified as being 100 percent correct for that specific vehicle.

Molded— Body and/or chassis seams that have been filled in or otherwise smoothed out.

Moons— Full wheel covers that are chrome and convex-shaped.

Muscle Car— A North American intermediate or mid-sized car produced between 1964 and 1972 (with a few exceptions) with a large displacement V-8 engine.

Nerf Bar— A custom-made bumper made of either solid or tubular stock and usually chromed.

Nitrous Oxide (N2O)— Also simply called nitrous, nitrous oxide is commonly known as laughing gas. Nitrous is often used in drag racing to boost engine performance for short periods. When burned, N_2O releases nitrogen and oxygen; the released oxygen permits more gasoline to be burned, resulting in the boost in power.

NHRA — This is an abbreviation for National Hot Rod Association.

NOS— This is an abbreviation for New Old Stock. Parts purchased from the manufacturer that were made at the time of the original vehicle but never sold.

Nosed— Chrome details and trim removed from the hood and smoothed over.

NSRA— This is an abbreviation for National Street Rod Association.

Original— Contains only parts originally installed on the car or NOS parts from the manufacturer with no substitute or aftermarket parts.

Piped— Narrow, padded pleats used to trim the interior.

Post— The pillar located between the front and rear doors of a four-door sedan.

Pro-Street— A vehicle that features large rear wheels and tires tucked deeply into the rear fender area.

Project Car— A car that is in restorable or customizable condition; raw material for a street rod.

Raked— The front end has been lowered more than the back; this term can also refer to a slanted windshield.

Replicar— A completed reproduction of an existing automotive design, usually sold only as a turn-key, or 100 percent complete, car.

Resto Rod— An original-looking car with a modified chassis, power plant, or drivetrain.

Roadster— A convertible without side windows; sometimes they don't even have tops.

Roll Pan— A smoothed panel that replaces the bumper and rolls back under the vehicle.

Rolled and Pleated— Deluxe interior sewn with padded pleats.

Rumble Seat— An open, fold-up rear seat located where the trunk would normally be.

Running Board— The metal strip running between the fenders and below the doors of early autos and trucks used as a step or to wipe one's feet before entering the vehicle.

Sectioned— Removing a horizontal section of bodywork to lower the overall height of the body.

Sedan Delivery— A two-door station wagon with solid body panels instead of windows on the sides at the back of the car.

Shaved— Door handles and body trim that have been removed and smoothed over.

Sidemount— A spare tire, recessed into the front fender.

Six-Pack— This is an engine equipped with three two-barrel carburetors, usually referring to Mopar vehicles.

Slammed— A significantly lowered vehicle—dropped as low as possible and still drivable.

Sleeper— A vehicle that doesn't look as fast as it is.

Split Window— This usually refers to the rear window—one that has two planes of glass with bodywork in between. The 1963 Corvette, for example, but many cars of the 1930s and 1940s had split windows, such as the 1935 Nash Aeroform.

Street Machine— A street-legal highly modified car or truck built in 1949 or later.

Suicide Door— A door that hinges at the rear and opens from the front.

upercharger— A crank-driven air-to-fuel mixture compressor which increases atmospheric pressure in the engine, resulting in added horsepower.

T-Bucket— A highly modified Ford Model T that is usually fenderless and topless. Most T-Buckets on the road today are kit cars or replicars.

Teardrops— Headlights that are round at the top and taper smoothly to a point at the bottom, resembling a tear drop. The stock 1937 Ford headlights are teardrops, for example.

TH— This is an abbreviation for Chevrolet Turbo Hydramatic transmissions. The TH350, TH400, and TH700R4 are all popular transmissions for street rods.

Trailer Queen— This is a derogatory term referring to a car that is transported to and from shows on or in a trailer and rarely, if ever, driven.

Tri-Power— This refers to an engine with three two-barrel carburetors, usually referring to GM vehicles.

Tubbed— Having the rear frame and body modified to allow for extra-wide wheels and tires that do not protrude past the fenders.

Tudor— This is a nickname for a two-door Ford sedan.

Tunneled— See "Frenched"—only deeper.

VIN— This is an abbreviation for Vehicle Identification Number. The vehicle serial number that is stamped onto the vehicle, usually under the windshield post, the driver's door post, or on the fire wall.

Vintage— A vehicle built between 1915 and 1942 in stock or unmodified condition.

Wheelie Bars— These are spring-mounted bars with rollers on their ends that protrude from the rear of a street rod that limit the height the front end can travel upward when pulling a "wheelie."

Woody— A woody is a vehicle that incorporates natural finished wood for structure of exposed body panels, such as the station wagons from the 1930s and 1940s that were frequently used by surfers to transport their surfboards.

Index

50 Years of Hot Rod
ISBN 0-7603-0575-7

**Best of Hot Rod Magazine
1949-1959**
ISBN 0-7603-1317-2

**Classic Customs
and Lead Sleds**
ISBN 0-7063-0851-9

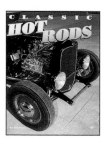

Classic Hot Rods
ISBN 0-7603-0721-0

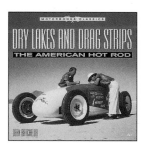

**Dry Lakes & Drag Strips:
The American Hot Rod**
ISBN 0-7603-1216-8

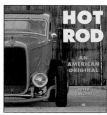

**Hot Rod:
An American Original**
ISBN 0-7603-0956-6

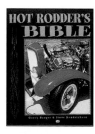

Hot Rodder's Bible
ISBN 0-7603-0767-9

Hot Rods – 500 Series
ISBN 0-7603-1435-7

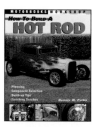

How to Build a Hot Rod
ISBN 0-7603-1304-0